BTRIPP BOOKS

BOOK REVIEWS FROM

2011

BY
BRENDAN TRIPP

These reviews originally appeared on the
"BTRIPP'S BOOKS" book review blog:
http://btripp-books.livejournal.com/

Copyright © 2016 by Brendan Tripp

ISBN 978-1-57353-411-6

An Eschaton Book

Front cover photo courtesy Kenn W. Kiser via morguefile.com.
Back cover photo courtesy Sebastian Santana via morguefile.com.

PREFACE

From 1993 through 2004, I ran the first manifestation of Eschaton Books (now in its third revival). Initially started as a vehicle to publish my poetry, it soon became evident that the market for poetry is vanishingly small, and in 1994 we "pivoted" into being a metaphysical press.

In this time, I was largely a one-man shop, doing everything from editorial to shipping, which was a huge time commitment, and I typically worked 14 hour days, 7 days a week to keep things moving. I bring up all this here because, despite having been a life-long avid reader, during this period I had precious little time for reading, and what reading I did get done was largely reviewing book submissions. However, I never stopped buying books, which began to stack up in prodigious "to be read" piles.

When Eschaton went out of business in 2004 (in a not unusual denouement for a small press – we had a distributor who ended up never paying us, while selling through all our stock), I found myself with a lot of reading to catch up on, and a need to keep my writing chops sharp. So, I began to pen little reviews of what I was reading through, and post those on the web.

As the years went by, this became "a thing" that I was doing, and, for a while, I was targeting a fairly aggressive goal of getting at least 72 non-fiction books read per year. By 2015, this had resulted in my having read and reviewed 700 books over that 12-year span.

In recent years (since the upswing in print-on-demand publishing), I have had numerous acquaintances suggest that I put out my reviews as books. I was, at first, rather hesitant on the concept (as, after all, the material was free to read on the web), but I eventually figured that if various people thought it was a good idea, I might as well give it a shot.

While I could have started at the beginning, with the reviews from 2004, I decided that those were less representative of the whole, so opted to begin with the most recent ones.

This 2011 collection is the fifth of these books, and gets a little deeper into that seven-year span where I was reading more that 72 books per year. There are, however, only 67 book reviews in this volume, which reflects the unpredictable gap (sometimes just a few days, sometimes a couple of months!) between when I finish reading the books and when I get around to cranking out the reviews.

As noted in the Preface to the 2012 book, the page count here is less than what it would be on later collections, as what I was targeting in terms of word-count on my reviews crept up over the past several years. I also was noticing, while pulling this together, that back then I used to typically insert just one blockquote from the text, while more recently I've had several, also making for longer books!

And, to repeat the note on my review "style": I do not write classic reviews, but more a telling of my personal interaction with a particular book. This means that I talk about where and how I got the book, how it relates to other things I've read, what sort of reactions it triggered in me (and why), and how one can get a copy if it sounds appealing. Needless to say, if the reader is devoted to standard book reviewing styles, this might be an irritation … however, it does make these reviews somewhat idiosyncratic to me, resulting in a collection that is something of a "my encounters with books" sort of deal, which will, hopefully, be of interest to many readers.

   - Brendan Tripp

CONTENTS

v -   Preface

vii - Contents

1 -   Saturday, January 22, 2011
>   *More essential reading ...*
>   **Switch: How to Change Things When Change Is Hard**
>   by Chip & Dan Heath

3 -   Sunday, January 23, 2011
>   *Uhhhh ... duuuude ...*
>   **The Seat of the Soul**
>   by Gary Zukav

5 -   Wednesday, January 26, 2011
>   *Now in Injia's sunny clime ...*
>   **Gunga Din and Other Favorite Poems**
>   by Rudyard Kipling

7 -   Thursday, January 27, 2011
>   *I keep having to remind myself, "it's a textbook" ...*
>   **Content Rules: How to Create Killer Blogs, Podcasts, Videos, Ebooks, Webinars (and More) That Engage Customers and Ignite Your Business**
>   by Ann Handley & C.C. Chapman

9 -   Saturday, February 5, 2011
>   *Bully! ... or just "bull"?*
>   **The Imperial Cruise:
>   A Secret History of Empire and War**
>   by James Bradley

11 - Sunday, February 6, 2011
>   *Social Media re-writing the marketing rulebook ...*
>   **Real-Time Marketing and PR: How to Instantly Engage Your Market, Connect with Customers, and Create Products that Grow Your Business Now**
>   by David Meerman Scott

13 - Sunday, February 13, 2011

A different approach to finding a job ...
**Cracking the Hidden Job Market:
How to Find Opportunity in Any Economy**
by Donald Asher

15 - Sunday, February 20, 2011

Makes me want to get on a plane ...
Realm of the Incas
by Victor W. Von Hagen

17 - Monday, February 21, 2011

Genesis, maybe ... Grail, not so much
Genesis of the Grail Kings
by Laurence Gardner

20 - Saturday, February 26, 2011

What do YOU want?
What Color Is Your Parachute? Job-Hunter's Workbook
by Richard N. Bolles

23 - Monday, February 28, 2011

I must see this sometime ...
The Importance of Being Earnest
by Oscar Wilde

25 - Saturday, March 5, 2011

Pointing ahead ...
The Thank You Economy
by Gary Vaynerchuk

28 - Sunday, March 6, 2011

Foreshadowing "Social Media" ...
**The Invisible Touch:
The Four Keys to Modern Marketing**
by Harry Beckwith

30 - Saturday, March 12, 2011

Quite a find ...
Zen Buddhism, An Introduction to Zen with Stories, Parables and Koan Riddles of the Zen Masters, Decorated with Figures from Old Chinese Ink-Paintings
by Peter Pauper Press

32 - Sunday, March 13, 2011

In search of the remarkable ...
Purple Cow: Transform Your Business by Being Remarkable
by Seth Godin

34 - Sunday, March 20, 2011

Valuable but frustrating ...
The Twelfth Insight: The Hour of Decision
by James Redfield

37 - Monday, March 21, 2011

Not for everybody ...
The NOW Revolution: 7 Shifts to Make Your Business Faster, Smarter and More Social
by Amber Naslund & Jay Baer

40 - Saturday, March 26, 2011

Be werry werry kwiet ...
On the Hunt: How to Wake Up Washington and Win the War on Terror
by Col. David Hunt

43 - Sunday, March 27, 2011

Hey, I'd settle for ONE!
50 Jobs in 50 States: One Man's Journey of Discovery Across America
by Daniel Seddiqui

46 - Saturday, April 2, 2011

Words of wisdom ...
An Open Heart: Practicing Compassion in Everyday Life
by H.H. The Dalai Lama

48 - Sunday, April 3, 2011

Just say no?
The Entrepreneur Equation: Evaluating the Realities, Risks, and Rewards of Having Your Own Business
by Carol Roth

51 - Saturday, April 9, 2011

Great stuff, but ...
Kahuna Magic
by Brad Steiger

53 - Sunday, April 10, 2011

Carry the news ...
Synchronicity: An Acausal Connecting Principle
by C.G. Jung

55 - Monday, April 25, 2011

From the Ferenginar exo-cultural archives ...
How Companies Win: Profiting from Demand-Driven Business Models No Matter What Business You're In
by Rick Kash & David Calhoun

57 - Sunday, May 1, 2011

Space songs on a spider web sitar ...
Sinagua Sunwatchers: An Archaeoastronomy Survey of the Sacred Mountain Basin
by Kenneth J. Zoll

59 - Monday, May 2, 2011

slowly disappearing from my view
Iran, The Green Movement and the USA: The Fox and the Paradox
by Hamid Dabashi

61 - Wednesday, May 4, 2011

An interesting take on things ...
A New Earth: Awakening to Your Life's Purpose
by Eckhart Tolle

64 - Monday, May 16, 2011

Changing your stories ...
Courageous Dreaming:
How Shamans Dream the World into Being
by Alberto Villoldo

66 - Tuesday, May 17, 2011

Glad to read somebody else's adventures ...
Jaguars Ripped My Flesh
by Tim Cahill

68 - Saturday, May 28, 2011

Framing the Mayan culture ...
Cities of the Maya in Seven Epochs,
1250 B.C. to A.D. 1903
by Steve Glassman & Armando Anaya

71 - Sunday, May 29, 2011

An AWESOME book for the job search!
What Color Is Your Parachute? Guide to Job-Hunting
Online, Sixth Edition: Blogging, Career Sites,
Gateways, Getting Interviews, Job Boards, Job Search
Engines, Personal Websites, Posting Resumes,
Research Sites, Social Networking
by Mark Emery Bolles

73 - Tuesday, May 31, 2011

A refreshing read ...
The Moral Landscape:
How Science Can Determine Human Values
by Sam Harris

76 - Monday, June 6, 2011

No, pie are ROUND!
A History of PI
by Petr Beckmann

79 - Tuesday, June 7, 2011

A French Curry?
Huna: Ancient Hawaiian Secrets for Modern Living
by Serge Kahili King

81 - Friday, June 17, 2011

My kind of town ...
**The Plan of Chicago: Daniel Burnham and
the Remaking of the American City**
by Carl Smith

83 - Sunday, June 19, 2011

Dead people's books ...
**Secret of the Forest:
On the Track of the Maya and Their Temples**
by Wolfgang Cordan

86 - Monday, June 27, 2011

I hear the train a'comin' ...
The Cluetrain Manifesto: The End of Business as Usual
by Rick Levine, Christopher Locke,
Doc Searls, & David Weinberger

89 - Saturday, July 9, 2011

What we're made of ...
The Human Genome: Book of Essential Knowledge
by John Quackenbush

91 - Sunday, July 10, 2011

The way these should have been ...
**The Celestine Vision:
Living the New Spiritual Awareness**
by James Redfield

93 - Saturday, July 16, 2011

Tibet is Tibet is Tibet ...
**Demystifying Tibet:
Unlocking the Secrets of the Land of the Snows**
by Lee Feigon

96 - Sunday, July 17, 2011

Sure as Kilimanjaro rises like Olympus above the Serengeti ...
**Surviving Your Serengeti:
7 Skills to Master Business and Life**
by Stefan Swanepoel

98 - Saturday, July 30, 2011

He asked, while shoving the Nunchuks under his jacket ...
**What Sticks: Why Most Advertising Fails
and How to Guarantee Yours Succeeds**
by Rex Briggs & Greg Stuart

100 - Sunday, July 31, 2011

None dare call it "seedy" ...
**The Seed:
Finding Purpose and Happiness in Life and Work**
by Jon Gordon

102 - Wednesday, August 3, 2011

Star light, star bright ...
**Keeper of Genesis:
A Quest for the Hidden Legacy of Mankind**
by Robert Bauval & Graham Hancock

104 - Saturday, August 20, 2011

80 things you should know ...
**Marketing Shortcuts for the Self-Employed:
Leverage Resources, Establish Online Credibility
and Crush Your Competition**
by Patrick Schwerdtfeger

107 - Sunday, August 21, 2011

The early Yeats ...
W. B. Yeats: Selected Poems
by William Butler Yeats

109 - Tuesday, August 23, 2011

Humor, history, and (reasonably) current events ...
Dave Barry's History of the Millennium (So Far)
by Dave Barry

111 - Sunday, August 28, 2011

Next she'll say he had no Katanas ...
**Beyond the Da Vinci Code:
From the Rose Line to the Bloodline**
by Sangeet Duchane

113 - Monday, August 29, 2011

What to do, what to do ...
101 Weird Ways to Make Money:
Cricket Farming, Repossessing Cars, and Other Jobs
With Big Upside and Not Much Competition
by Steve Gillman

115 - Thursday, September 1, 2011

Theravada training ...
Beyond the Stream of the World
by Phra Ācariya Thoon Khippapañño

117 - Sunday, September 11, 2011

Hard to believe ...
The Pearl of Great Price
by Joseph Smith

120 - Wednesday, September 14, 2011

A peek behind the curtains ...
Our Life with Mr. Gurdjieff
by Thomas & Olga de Hartmann

123 - Saturday, October 22, 2011

Picture this ...
Going Pro: How to Make the Leap
from Aspiring to Professional Photographer
by Scott Bourne & Skip Cohen

125 - Sunday, October 23, 2011

A time to rend, a time to sew
Rhetoric and Kairos:
Essays in History, Theory, and Praxis
by Phillip Sipiora & James S. Baumlin

127 - Monday, October 24, 2011

This is a fun book ...
God, No!: Signs You May Already Be an Atheist
and Other Magical Tales
by Penn Jillette

129 - Tuesday, October 25, 2011

Counting on it ...
**The Man of Numbers:
Fibonacci's Arithmetic Revolution**
by Keith Devlin

131 - Wednesday, October 26, 2011

Like a cyclone ranger ...
Japanese Religion, Unity and Diversity
by H. Byron Earhart

133 - Tuesday, November 1, 2011

Unlocking Secrets ...
The Master Key to Riches
by Napoleon Hill

136 - Friday, November 4, 2011

An intense and hopeless despair ...
Heart of Darkness
by Joseph Conrad

138 - Saturday, November 5, 2011

The other side of the story ...
Narrative of the Life of Frederick Douglass
by Frederick Douglass

141 - Sunday, November 6, 2011

Kept waiting for them to call me "maggot" ...
Guerrilla Marketing for Job Hunters
by Jay Conrad Levinson & David E. Perry

144 - Tuesday, November 8, 2011

Outside the norm ...
Outliers: The Story of Success
by Malcolm Gladwell

147 - Tuesday, November 22, 2011

Not just for marketers ...
**Grab More Market Share: How to Wrangle Business
Away from Lazy Competitors**
by Ross Shafer

150 - Sunday, November 27, 2011

And, what IS reality?
Changing Reality
by Serge Kahili King

153 - Monday, November 28, 2011

A "feel good" business book ...
Start Something That Matters
by Blake Mycoskie

155 - Thursday, December 29, 2011

So much depends on context ...
Situations Matter:
Understanding How Context Transforms Your World
by Sam Sommers

158 - Saturday, December 31, 2011

A splendid book ..
What Is God?
by Jacob Needleman

161 - **QR Code Links**

181 - **Contents - Alphabetical By Author**

187 - **Contents - Alphabetical By Title**

Saturday, January 22, 2011[1]

More essential reading ...

This book came into my hands via a fairly unusual route, although one that I'm always happy to encounter. A sponsor (in this case on-line educator Ashford University) had picked up on one of those ever-more-frequent deals being offered by publishers that if they bought X# of books, the publisher would provide the author as an event speaker. I had stumbled over info on this somewhere (could have been an invite, could have been a newsletter, heck, could have been the EventBrite listings) and signed up for the early morning session featuring the Dan half of the Chip & Dan Heath authoring duo. I was pleasantly surprised to encounter a very nice breakfast up at the Mid-America Club, and finding that we were being given free (and autographed, if we made the effort) copies of Switch: How to Change Things When Change Is Hard[2]. Score!

I feel somewhat bad that I waited the better part of a year before getting around to reading this, as the presentation by Mr. Heath was quite engaging. However, it is one of those books that seemed somewhere in-between my typical reading genres, too much of a "business book" when I was interested in reading something less staid, and too "off topic" if I was trying to get something done for inclusion in The Job Stalker[3] blog. As it turned out, neither of these concerns were particularly true for Switch[4], as it is really about general psychological realities, and approaches to managing them, so it had the interest level typical of a non-business book, but was applicable to the job search.

Key to the Heaths' thesis here is that there are two competing aspects in our minds, the rational and the emotional sides, for which they borrowed Jonathan Haidt's terminology of "The Rider" and "The Elephant", one which very much wants to lose 30lbs, and one that simultaneously wants to finish off the rest of the pack of cookies.

I have probably mentioned previously how much I very, very, *very* much hate "emotional appeals" in ads and elsewhere (I gave up listening to an otherwise enjoyable radio station because the ads running on it were predictably emotional quagmires featuring pitches to greed, envy, fear, desire, etc. rather than information about their products or services), along the lines of one of the classic *A-Team* quotes: *"That's not a smile; that's just a bunch of teeth messin' with my mind!"*. What is really remarkable about Switch[5] is that it not only *explained* what was going on in what I had always considered to be egregiously dishonest sales pitches, but to even *embrace* the use of emotional content in certain contexts.

One of the key perceptions here (and most of the material in the book is supported by studies of various types) is that "The Elephant" is fairly tireless, but "The Rider" has a very limited span of time where it's able to be in control (in one study, subjects who had been faced with a "resisting temptation" side-issue before a difficult challenge, only managed to stay on-task before giving up for *eight minutes*, as opposed to the *nineteen minutes* managed by the non-tempted subjects!), suggesting that "self control" is a very scarce resource, which can be easily spent in unexpected ways.

Not only is "The Rider" only able to muster a certain amount of self-control, it is also subject to "decision paralysis". The Heaths detail situations where doctors in a study where only half as likely to opt for a non-surgical option if there were two drugs to choose from rather than just one, where food stores sampling stations produced *ten times* the sales when they offered six products rather than 24 (how counter-intuitive is *that*?), and similar results in situations as divergent as HR materials on 401k plans and speed-dating events!

Switch[6] not only looks at these situations, but it provides a "game plan" for creating change. This breaks down into three elements, each with three actions:

> "Direct the Rider":
> > "Follow the Bright Spots"
> > "Script the Critical Moves"
> > "Point to the Destination"
> "Motivate the Elephant":
> > "Find the Feeling"
> > "Shrink the Change"
> > "Grow your People"
> "Shape the Path":
> > "Tweak the Environment"
> > "Build Habits"
> > "Rally the Herd"

While a "9-point plan" may seem somewhat intimidating in itself, all the factors here are supported with material from a wide range of cultures and settings (from customer service at Rackspace to societal change in Tanzania), and the approach breaks down into sufficiently manageable chunks that anyone should be able to use this in pretty much any area of their life. Although not addressed in the book, those who have read Gurdjieff will find the three-phase approach here echoing the "foods" of the Physical, Emotional, and Intellectual centers in his system … so there's even a metaphysical aspect to this read.

Needless to say, I'm quite enthusiastic about Switch[7], and I would heartily recommend it to anybody. While it's been out for nearly a year, it doesn't appear to have shaken down into the used market much (I can understand people wanting to keep their copies!), so your best bet is likely via Amazon which, at this writing, has the hardcover edition available for nearly half-off, which is only a smidge more than what the new/used vendors (less, if you figure in adding this to something else to get free shipping). Again, this is a good one, and you should check it out.

Notes:
1. http://btripp-books.livejournal.com/104649.html
2. http://amzn.to/1VkA8vH
3. http://jobstalker.info/
4-7. http://amzn.to/1VkA8vH

Sunday, January 23, 2011[1]

Uhhhh ... duuuude ...

Every now and again I hit a book that I *anticipated* really liking, and find that the reality runs counter to the anticipation, and I have to wonder *"is it ME or is it the book?"*. In this case I'm not sure which one it is, but there was a definite disconnect. I'd picked this up via one of B&N's clearance sales (which I've come to realize do not mean that the book is out of print, as this is still available for order) for $1.99 ... and was having "warm fuzzies" about getting it, having read *The Dancing Wu Li Masters* "back in the day" ... however, whether it's me ceasing to be a starry-eyed youth, or the author descending into a newagey morass, I'm not sure.

However, reading Gary Zukav's The Seat of the Soul[2] reminded me nothing so much as hanging out with intelligent, but deeply dope-addicted, friends in college and listening to them ramble on about spiritual matters based on little more than the effects of the weed. Sure, they had some bits and pieces thrown into their discourse based on solid research and/or meditative experience, but most of it seemed to be flying "off the cuff" in the moment. This book is like 250 pages of that.

As suggested in the above, this does not mean that there is *nothing* of value in this, it's just that filtering out what is worthwhile is quite a challenge given the level that most of this is at. One main part of this book is the difference between the "five-sensory human" and the "multisensory personality" contrasting the two with attention to "external power" vs. "authentic power" ... these dichotomies weave through the book, but go on such rollercoaster rides that it's very difficult to walk away from the reading with any concrete understanding of what the author's getting at. I guess for a certain "newagey" audience this suffices, but it really does sound like the herb talking.

Rather than trying to provide a cogent over-view of something which does not seem to be particularly amenable to this approach, I'll throw out some quotes here:

> We are evolving from five-sensory humans into multisensory humans. Our five senses, together, form a single sensory system that is designed to perceive physical reality. The perceptions of a multisensory human extend beyond physical reality to the larger dynamical systems of which our physical reality is a part. The multisensory human is able to perceive and to appreciate, the role that our physical reality plays in a larger picture of evolution, and the dynamics by which our physical reality is creat-

> ed and sustained. This realm is invisible to the five-sensory human.
>
> ...
>
> To the five-sensory personality, intuitive insights, or hunches, occur unpredictably, and cannot be counted upon. To the multisensory personality, intuitive insights are registrations within its consciousness of a loving guidance that is continually assisting and supporting its growth. Therefore, the mutisensory personality strives to increase its awareness of this guidance.
>
> The first step to this is becoming aware of what you are feeling. Following your feeling will lead you to their source. Only through emotions can you encounter the force field of your own soul. That is the human passage in a word.
>
> ...
>
> Temptation is the Universe's compassionate way of allowing you to run through what would be a harmful negative karmic dynamic if you were to allow it to become physically manifest. It is the energy through which your soul is given the gracious opportunity to have a dry run at a life lesson, at a situation that, if you can see clearly, can be removed and healed within the confines of your private world of energy and not spill into a larger energy field of other souls. Temptation is a dress rehearsal for a karmic experience of negativity.

While there are good, perhaps even *profound* perceptions cropping up at various points here, most of it is dense, hazy, and ill-defined, and swings between discussions of things from animals to diet, with sweeping assertions presented without a shred of what would be called (in a "five-sensory" context, I suppose) *evidence*. Again, the general tenor of the book is of being stuck in a seemingly endless (I kept aching to get done with reading this!) discussion with your favorite pot-headed friend.

Of course if the above quotes sound great to you … you'll probably find The Seat of the Soul[3] your cup of tea (or some other leafy product), but for most, it's not worth the time it will take to plow through. If you *do* think that this sounds like something that you'd be interested in subjecting yourself to, you should certainly take up the new/used guy's deals, as "like new" copies of the hardcover are available for a penny (four bucks with shipping).

Notes:

1. http://btripp-books.livejournal.com/104912.html
2-3. http://amzn.to/1R9rOyT

Wednesday, January 26, 2011[1]

Now in Injia's sunny clime ...

Here's another "fill in the gaps in my education" read ... as while I certainly *encountered* Kipling in the course of completing an English Major (heck, I had the two volumes of the massive Norton Anthology of English Literature as texts in both high school and college), I don't specifically recall ever having sat down to *read* any of his writings aside what had filtered through in the appropriate classes. As is often the case with these "fill in" books, this is a Dover Thrift Edition, one of those marvelous small books with marvelously small cover prices which I frequently use to turn a $23.48 book order into an over-$25 book order with free shipping, nearly always saving more than the cost of the book!

Gunga Din and Other Favorite Poems[2] by Rudyard Kipling is a collection of 44 of his poems, organized by the collection in which they had originally been published, from 1886 though 1912. In it are his well-known pieces such as the title poem, "The White Man's Burden" and "The Female of the Species", all of which are certainly a window into another time ... no doubt one viewed with dismay bordering on horror by those of the "politically correct" stripe. These are poems written at the height of the British Empire, and crafted to speak to the English of the age. One aspect of this I really hadn't expected (although, had I recalled more of *Gunga Din*, I would have), was his use of "colloquial voices", imitating the patois of the British common man, or more usually, common soldier. An example of this comes from "The 'Eathen":

> *The young recruit is 'appy*
> *– 'e throws his chest to suit;*
>
> *You see 'im grow mustaches;*
> *you 'ear 'im slap 'is boot;*
>
> *'E learns to drop the "bloodies"*
> *from every word he slings,*
>
> *An 'e shows an 'ealthy brisket*
> *when 'e strips for bars an' rings.*

A significant portion of these poems are written in this mode, no doubt increasing their popularity at the time, but making their impact a bit muddled today, unless read out loud!

Not all these are about the adventures of Empire, many are simply about the human condition, in various states. This part of the poem "Tomlinson", about a man too bad for Hell, particularly grabbed me both for its crafting and for its cosmology:

> *The Spirit gripped him by the hair,*
> *and sun by sun they fell*
>
> *Till they came to the belt of Naughty Stars*
> *that rim the mouth of Hell:*
>
> *The first are red with pride and wrath,*
> *the next are white with pain,*
>
> *But the third are black with clinkered sin*
> *that cannot burn again:*
>
> *They may hold their path,*
> *they may leave their path,*
> *with never a soul to mark,*
>
> *They may burn or freeze,*
> *but they must not cease*
> *in the Scorn of the Outer Dark.*
>
> *The Wind that blows between the worlds,*
> *it nipped him to the bone,*
>
> *And he yearned to the flare of Hell-gate*
> *there as the light of his own hearth-stone.*
>
> *The Devil he sat behind the bars,*
> *where the desperate legions drew,*
>
> *But he caught the hasting Tomlinson*
> *and would not let him through.*

Anyway, Gunga Din[3] was an interesting trip into late Victorian English life, and especially into the far-flung outposts of the British Empire and the "grunts" who made sure the sun didn't set on the Union Jack.

As noted above, this is a Dover Thrift book, with a whopping $2.00 cover price. It is unlikely, given the slim mark-up on such a book, that you'll find it at your local brick-and-mortar book seller, but it is one of those things handy to have ready to push an on-line order into the free-shipping promised land!

Notes:

1. http://btripp-books.livejournal.com/105121.html

2-3. http://amzn.to/1S9syis

Thursday, January 27, 2011[1]

I keep having to remind myself, "it's a textbook" ...

This was another of those books that came to me from the good folks at Wiley as a review copy, no doubt in anticipation of being featured in my The Job Stalker[2] blog over on the Tribune's "Chicago Now" site (which I figure it will be next Monday). This is the fifth book in their "New Rules of Social Media" series, three of which I've been happy to get for review (why I didn't see the other two, I don't know!). I was informed, following a somewhat middling review of Get Seen[3] that these were being designed for use as text books, which goes a long way to explaining why they are considerably less engaging than other books in the Social Media sphere, and I have since gone into reading these with that particular piece of info in mind.

Which brings me to a bit of a conflict. I have heard and read numerous *rave* reviews and commentary on Ann Handley & C.C. Chapman's Content Rules: How to Create Killer Blogs, Podcasts, Videos, Ebooks, Webinars (and More) That Engage Customers and Ignite Your Business[4], and yet I was unable to work up much enthusiasm for it. I mean, it certainly is a *good* book, and might well be an excellent entry-point for somebody otherwise clueless about Social Media, but it lacks *life* ... just as there is a world of difference between a historical survey of the French revolution and Victor Hugo's Les Misérables, this, unfortunately, seems as flat as the former when stacked up against something like Scott Stratten's UnMarketing[5]! Of course, if one reflects that one is "reading a textbook", this might be expected, but I still don't know where *other folks'* excitement comes from.

In any case, Content Rules[6] is a very solid book that walks the reader through various aspects of the Social Media landscape, and is illustrated with examples of how several companies have used the techniques under discussion to achieve successes. At its best, this is a "framework" for developing a Social Media strategy, featuring numerous lists and checklists for putting one's *"we should be doing some of this social media stuff!"* desires into a clear plan. First of these are "The Content Rules":

1. Embrace being a publisher.
2. Insight inspires originality.
3. Build momentum.
4. Speak human.
5. Reimagine; don't recycle.
6. Share or solve; don't shill.
7. Show; don't just tell.
8. Do something unexpected.
9. Stoke the campfire.
10. Create wings and roots.
11. Play to your strengths.

Not surprisingly, these are also the chapter headings for the first section of the book, as the authors discuss each of these "rules". This part is somewhat "philosophical" in that it's explaining why these "rules" are "rules", but it also has several very handy lists, ranging from this one about one's audience:

1. Whom are you trying to reach?
2. Where do they spend their time online?
3. How do they access the web?
4. What are they craving?
5. What do you want them to do?
6. What content do you already have?

... on to a *twenty-five point list* answering the question *"What Do I Talk About When There's Nothing To Say?"*!

The second part of the book is "The How-To Section", which has chapters on blogs, webinars, ebooks/whitepapers, case studies, FAQs, videos, podcasting, and photos. Needless to say, this is the "meat" of the book, with overviews of these assorted vehicles, a look at why they may or may not be good for your situation, and step-by-step outlines of how to use each (and even a fill-in-the-blanks template for setting up a blog, for the writing-averse). A third section looks at the efforts of 10 organizations, large and small, with a chapter each on how they solved a particular problem by using Social Media, including an "Ideas You Can Steal" feature highlighting key techniques. A final fourth "section" (it's only 3 pages long) gives you URLs to web-based additional content an a "12-point checklist" for Social Media.

Again, there's nothing *wrong* with Content Rules[7], and many people are *very* complimentary towards it, but it never quite grabbed me. If you're a Social Media practitioner, this is likely to be less-than-inspiring, but might be a good book to drop on the desk of a boss/colleague who's a "non-believer", or to send to a potential client to spark some ideas. There were a few bits in here that I bookmarked to go back to for some ideas, but it's not likely one that I'm planning on re-reading.

As this is brand new, you have a pretty good shot at finding it at a brick-and-mortar store that carries Social Media sorts of titles, but Amazon has it (at this writing) at a fairly substantial (37%) discount which makes it quite affordable. If you're looking for an introductory book on Social Media, either for yourself or for somebody else, this would be a very capable primer, but mind my reactions if you're familiar with the field and looking for a rah-rah book to get excited about.

Notes:
1. http://btripp-books.livejournal.com/105288.html
2. http://jobstalker.info/
3. http://btripp-books.livejournal.com/90126.html
4. http://amzn.to/21Jqoev
5. http://btripp-books.livejournal.com/101421.html
6-7. http://amzn.to/21Jqoev

Saturday, February 5, 2011[1]

Bully! ... or just "bull"?

Here's another book "snagged" from the LibraryThing.com Early Reviewers program. I was somewhat surprised when I "won" this (see details here[2]), as I really haven't read that many political history books recently, so the LTER's "Almighty Algorithm" must have been digging into the older levels of my library[3] when it matched me up with this book.

It's hard to know where to start on James Bradley's The Imperial Cruise: A Secret History of Empire and War[4]. The author certainly has credits to his name, including the book on which the movie *Flags of our Fathers* was based, but this book is *such* "a shock to the system" in relation to standard-issue American History, that one has to wonder how solid this is, or how wildly spun ... or not. There has been a lot of hostility towards it (check out the couple of hundred reviews of it on Amazon, where a plurality, at 40% of the total, give it only *one* star!), with the general consensus being that the author had a particular (somewhat leftist) axe to grind, and that the resulting book is more of an attack piece than an actual "history". Against this perception are the over 800 citations pointing to source materials from the time.

What time, you ask? Who is being attacked? This is a book about Teddy Roosevelt, his life, his personality, his rise to power, and what he did when he got it. And, it's a book about *race* and racial theories, especially those of turn-of-the-century America (notably, there is *nothing* directly commenting on just how radically changed the question of race has become over the past 50 years, which may indicate a certain "blind spot" of the author's). According to this book, Roosevelt was driven by a view of race that was prevalent in the Universities and halls of government at the time, based on a vision of the Teutonic Aryan sweeping away "degenerate races" as they followed the Sun westward around the planet, reflected in books such as Types of Mankind[5], which appears to have been a *standard scientific text* at the time.

According to the author, Roosevelt also had little respect for the structures of a democratic republic, as much of the book is about him running assorted secret negotiations (and campaigns) in which every effort was made to keep Congress "out of the loop". The central piece of the book (and source of the title) was when he sent his daughter, Alice (sort of the Princess Di of her day) as the "star" of a massive outreach featuring William Howard Taft and several other dignitaries, on a "cruise" to Asia in 1905.

The central thesis of The Imperial Cruise[6] is that Roosevelt created the conditions in the Pacific Rim that later "bore fruit" in an aggressive Japan in World War 2 (indeed, the author suggests that the attack on Pearl Harbor was a copy-cat ploy based on our own first moves on the Spanish in the Philippines), a destabilized Korea, leading to the Korean War, and even

Vietnam, with Ho Chi Minh initially believing that America would come to the aide of a native revolution. Bradley argues that Roosevelt's unwavering belief in White destiny would allow him to sweep into country after country and simply eliminate the populations, much like earlier generations and leaders (going back to Jefferson) had done with the Native Americans.

The picture painted here was that there was no *shame*, no *doubt* that a genocidal policy was not only justified (in the "superior culture" eradicating the "inferior culture"), but *RIGHT*, being the course of a Natural Law no less "obvious" than gravity. If this was what Roosevelt *believed*, he used the vision of a "benevolent and fair" American government "coming to the aid" of various native peoples being oppressed by the Colonial powers (particularly Spain) as the premise for "following the Sun". According to this, Roosevelt was careful to never have his emissaries make any promises *in writing*, all negotiations were done "on his word" as that of the American people, which provided, time and again, a convenient way to simply have his way once the U.S. was in place. After all, *"Victorious American Aryans had no intention of handing a state to [an] inferior race."*, and in every case, Cuba, Central and South America, Hawaii/Polynesia, the Philippines, each except that of Japan, it was "meet the new (White) boss; same as the old (White) boss" or a new level of rapacious Christian Missionary plantation developers which brought worse conditions that the previous colonial rule.

Very little of this has, obviously, filtered into the "standard history" taught to us in school, and I found myself *wishing* that this was all an over-the-top polemic by an "internationalist" Leftist with a Michelle Obama-like view of America. However, if even a portion of this is *true*, it's quite a shocking eye-opener to how we've conducted foreign policy.

The Imperial Cruise[7] is, as one would take from the above, *not* a particularly pleasant read, although it's written engagingly enough. While this would certainly *appeal* more to the anti-American Left, it's also a book that conservatives should read, if just to see something of themselves reflected in a none-too-complimentary mirror. Personally speaking, I'm as "Teutonic" a W.A.S.P. as they come, and I was *mortified* by this book, as against the grain of "Mayflower Society orthodoxy" as it is. It also shows just how far the country has moved in the direction that it has moved over the past century.

This book is "new" in the paperback, being a "reprint edition" of the previous hardcover. Due to this, it's probably more affordable to pick up than most of the "Early Reviewer" books. At this writing, Amazon has this new at 43% off, putting it down to the level that the used copies of the previous release are (with shipping). I don't know what the brick-and-mortar places have this at, but it should be out there. Again, this is either going to horrify you or confirm your political views, but on either side of the question, it's an interesting look at a very different time in our country.

Notes:
1. http://btripp-books.livejournal.com/105712.html
2. http://goo.gl/5CmQU4
3. http://btripp-books.com/
4. http://amzn.to/1hUENEG
5. http://goo.gl/PuXiqk
6-7. http://amzn.to/1hUENEG

Sunday, February 6, 2011[1]

Social Media re-writing the marketing rulebook ...

This is another book sent out to me by the good folks at Wiley. Since I've been in the Social Media arena for quite a while (in various permutations, both professionally and personally), I've seen many books from them, this being a niche in which they're quite active. As regular readers know, I also write a job-search blog over on the Chicago Tribune's "ChicagoNow" site, The Job Stalker[2], which features stories from my own (now 20-month-old) job search, tips and tricks I've amassed from *previous* job searches, materials that I've found via Twitter, etc., and book reviews that I find "on target" for that audience. I bring this point up because it was only *now*, sitting down to write this review, that it really occurred to me that David Meerman Scott's book Real-Time Marketing and PR: How to Instantly Engage Your Market, Connect with Customers, and Create Products that Grow Your Business Now[3] is specifically a book addressing *businesses*, rather than individuals ... my confusion no doubt coming from my own immersion in "marketing & PR" and the social media field. This is going to involve some "tap dancing" on Monday, where I've slated a blog post on this over there!

I realized part way through this that I've been following Scott on Twitter (@dmscott[4]) for a while, so had a certain familiarity with him, even though I'd not read his previous books (and he has some fascinating ones, such as *Marketing Lessons from the Grateful Dead*). In this volume he endeavors to re-define the business use of Social Media and its various forms as "Real-Time" efforts. The book starts with the iconic case of the viral video "United Breaks Guitars"[5] in which a band, whose guitars were trashed in transit by United Airlines (you didn't see *that* coming, did you?), had run through all the "official channels" for complaint resolution, hit a brick wall, and resorted to music and the internet to make a statement. Almost everybody who "lives on the web" has seen this video at this point ... what is notable here is how Scott tracks the dynamics of the data for the *spread* of this video, both on YouTube and on various blogs talking about it, quantifying the "viral" of its spread. On top of this, he brings up factors that were *new to me*, about how both the maker of the broken guitars in question, and a maker of guitar *cases*, reacted within hours to take advantage of the buzz by affiliating themselves with the aggrieved party, while the "dinosaur" corporation took nearly *two months* to make a substantial response. The rest of the book lays out what *needs* to be done, what tools are out there, and how these tools can best be applied to a wide spectrum of emergencies and opportunities *as they happen*.

Real-Time Marketing & PR[6] is laid out in three sections, "Revolution Time" which looks at all the elements of the Social Media and web world, how these can affect one's business, and how one can deal with them; "Connect With Your Market" which, not surprisingly, shows how to reach out to one's assorted audiences and make the "real-time" connection with them; and "Grow Your Business Now" which shows ways to make these connections turn into sales, etc. The book is filled with specific examples, both good and bad, from real-life situations that companies have faced, and these are sufficiently gripping that I never noticed that I was reading a "business book"!

Much of what @dmscott[7] focuses on here is how large companies (such as United) have to have substantial cultural shifts to be able to successfully work in "real-time" situations. These days things can get significantly out of control if they're not *immediately* dealt with (a recent example is how Taco Bell defused the "35% beef" meme with a counter-message detailing the actual, 88%, content of their products). It requires putting a LOT of trust and responsibility in the hands of "front line" people who can "make things right" *now*, not after six levels of meetings, and word back from the lawyers. Obviously, huge corporations can't become small flexible start-ups, but they can develop structures where small, flexible, *teams* have the ability to act that way, and strategies for this are outlined here.

Real-Time Marketing & PR[8] is brand new (it's been out since November, despite its 2011 copyright notice), and so should be at your local book vendor that carries business books. It is also currently at a fairly deep discount at Amazon (48% off!) which makes it the best bet for the moment. Again, this is a book for businesses, but it's also a very good read for individuals who are in (or want to be in) the social media "real-time" sphere. I enjoyed this very much, and look forward to catching up with other of Scott's books, and would recommend this to anybody with an interest in this area!

Notes:

1. http://btripp-books.livejournal.com/105905.html
2. http://jobstalker.info/
3. http://amzn.to/1S9qozf
4. http://twitter.com/dmscott
5. http://www.youtube.com/watch?v=5YGc4zOqozo
6. http://amzn.to/1S9qozf
7. http://twitter.com/dmscott
8. http://amzn.to/1S9qozf

Sunday, February 13, 2011[1]

A different approach to finding a job ...

The current volume comes to me courtesy of the good folks at Ten Speed Press, who obviously felt that Donald Asher's Cracking the Hidden Job Market: How to Find Opportunity in Any Economy[2] would be a good fit with my The Job Stalker[3] blog over on the Tribune's "Chicago Now" site. Considering that I've been doing "book features" over there on all sorts of social media topics of late, it certainly *will be* a "return to subject"!

Those following along at home will realize that my own job search has somewhat stalled following the "one of three finalists" situation I had back in November, followed by an intensive burst of freelance work. It was from these doldrums that I approached Mr. Asher's book (I should say "latest book" as he has another dozen[4] titles in print). The author has a high-end consultancy for executives between jobs, and has developed the "HJM" approach in this book from his work over the years with these clients.

While none of this is ground-breaking in the finer granularity of particular tasks, it is organized into an approach that allows the job seeker to systematically work through its elements, and this system is a good deal different than anything that I've read. One thing the author doesn't do is coddle the reader, at many points in Cracking the Hidden Job Market[5] he sounds positively drill-sergeant insistent on what one should and should not be doing. Key to these is to not hide behind a keyboard and just fire off resumes to posted jobs, and #1 on the "to do" list is: *Talk to people!*

Parts of this will be difficult for various types. As I've noted, I'm *equally* plausible to be working in any of five or six quite distinct roles within the wider "communications" umbrella, having successfully held these jobs at various points in my career. One of the more difficult things he focuses on here for me is to figure out a maximum of *three* job titles, and only go looking for those specific positions. I guess I've "never figured out what I want to be when I grow up", so I find that level of filtering very difficult to do (which has proved a stumbling block in many other job-search "systems"), and would really prefer a position where I "wear many hats". This divergence initially put me off on the book, but the "action elements" here were sufficiently strong that he eventually won me back over, even if I'd have to do a "dartboard selection" for a career goal.

The major difficulty that I think most folks are likely to find with this is the notion that one needs to have at least 100 *leads* active at all times. This takes dedication, drive, organization, and a lot of *work* to develop. The "job seekers" who spend most of the week on the couch with a remote in their hand are not likely to be inclined to gear up to this task (the "average job seeker" spends only *six* hours a week actively looking for a job, Asher suggests a "full-time schedule" of 8 hours M-Th, plus a half-day each on Friday morning and Sunday afternoon, plus a Sunday-night session with a 15-point "scorecard" to assess what you've achieved in the week).

The key element that keeps coming up throughout Cracking the Hidden Job Market[6] is getting into face-to-face meetings with people who may lead to jobs. This differs from the "networking" model (that I've been applying) in that it's not just being out and rubbing elbows with folks, but actively contacting people and setting up meetings, be they in an office setting, over a cup of coffee, or a breakfast or lunch. Having a focused target and constant in-person activity to move towards that target appear to be the main points in the "HJM" system.

One thing that also set the material in this book apart from others is the author's insistence on *being insistent*. calling multiple times a day (not leaving more than one voicemail, but making the phone ring), *re-sending* e-mails that have not garnered a reply, and ways to get around recalcitrant "gatekeepers". As far as calling goes, he even says *"Call once a day until one of you dies"*!

While he does counsel insistence, he doesn't suggest bashing one's head against the wall, and there are many situations where one might be looking for the wrong job in the wrong place with the wrong experience. If a dozen or so different folks you've met with tell you it's not happening, it might very well be the case (I think the example he used was for a welder wanting to get into high-fashion photography while living in Des Moines), and you should probably adjust some elements of your search (he is very pro-relocation here).

Asher gives examples of various folks that he's worked with, and many of these, applying these principles, made transitions in a matter of *weeks* … but the key is getting to the folks who are hiring *before* the jobs are posted, possibly even before the hiring manager has actually set up a job. One technique he suggests is calling up some identified contact at a company and saying "*I wonder if you're thinking about hiring a #####. Who would I talk to about that?*"… you either get blown off or you get referred to somebody closer to hiring you. One of the lines that stood out in one of the many "action lists" here is "*Repeat until hired.*", do the proper activities in the proper sequence, and with enough repetition, they should result in that job. After all, you're only looking for *one* job, and if you push through enough targeted activity, it's the only sale that matters.

Anyway, Cracking the Hidden Job Market[7] has only been out since the start of the year, so should be on the shelves of the brick-and-mortar book vendors who carry job-search books. It has a very reasonable cover price, and at the moment Amazon has it at about 1/3rd off, which makes it a very small price to pay for what could completely change your job search.

Notes:
1. http://btripp-books.livejournal.com/106017.html
2. http://amzn.to/1S9pOSc
3. http://jobstalker.info/
4. http://goo.gl/fwcdQ7
5-7. http://amzn.to/1S9pOSc

Sunday, February 20, 2011

Makes me want to get on a plane ...

Over the years, I've come to be *less* creeped out by having "dead people's books", as my economic situation over the past decade or so has greatly favored obtaining used copies. Of course, there are *used* copies and there are copies which are pretty clearly available due to the expiring of their original owner. Generally speaking, the books at the Newberry Library Book Fair are of the latter sort, and, while a fascinating source of perhaps otherwise-unavailable volumes, there is frequently a fairly clear awareness that this "was somebody else's" before finding its way into my library.

In the case of Realm of the Incas[2] by Victor W. Von Hagen, I'm happy that it was available. Von Hagen was an explorer of Central and South America who published several dozen books on archaeological and anthropological topics in the 40's, 50's, and 60's, many in very inexpensive mass market paperback editions, so I'm guessing he was quite widely read in those decades. Given this output, I find it fascinating that it appears only *one* of these volumes (a book on the Maya) got reissued in a later edition (in the 90's). The current title was initially published n 1957, and the copy I have is from the seventh printing in 1963 (it's interesting how many scans of this are out there with various now-amazingly-low cover prices, this one having originally been priced at 60¢!).

As long-time readers may recall, I've traveled/studied in South America in the past, so I had a certain context for this book, and have read a modicum of historical books (aside from the shamanic and indigenous learning material) on the subject, and *my impression* of Realm of the Incas[3] is that it brings the history and culture of the Incas to life more than any other book of its kind has. Of course, going in, with the evolving nature of archaeological/anthropological research, one has to wonder how much the "general knowledge" from half a century ago has held up over that time.

It appears that Von Hagen's specialty was in the study of roads (he has titles on other road systems and mentioned particular expeditions in this), and certainly that's a great place to start when looking at the Incas. Back in the 80's I was fortunate to be able to be on a program in which we hiked "the Inca Trail" from Cuzco to Machu Picchu, so I had a certain familiarity with this, and even with some of locations discussed. However, this was only one aspect of this look at Peru's great empire.

The book in in four sections, a historical background where pre-Inca cultures are noted (the Inca were a fairly late evolution in their region, from vague origins around 1,000 CE through the Spanish conquest and consolidation of control in the mid-1,500's), a look at the Inca people and their environment in 16 specific elements (ranging from the *Allyu*, a community structure still in use with the natives, to the *Mita*, the "service tax" imposed on the people), a consideration of the person of the Inca and the capital at Cuzco, and, lastly, a look at the Incan cultural achievements, from the notable architecture to the *Quipu* system of record-keeping via knots in cords.

Again, I am hesitant to "speak for the research" here, given that the author covers so wide a spectrum of elements (on which he could hardly be an expert across the board), and that he was an "adventurer" writing in the 50's (where aspects might well have been "romanced" to a certain extent), but most of this rings true from my experience and background on the subject, and he certainly "brings it to life" more than most.

Given this, I'm somewhat amazed that Realm of the Incas[4] did not seem to have a printing past 1963, and I'm wondering why his other forty-some-odd books have likewise not been re-issued (books published through 1963 might well be in public domain at this point, if the copyright owner wasn't actively renewing it). However, I was also pleased to see that there are quite a lot of used copies, even up to "like new" (the one I got at Newberry was probably no better than "good"), for very little … in fact, one of the Amazon new/used guys has a "like new" copy of this for just a penny (plus, of course, the $3.99 shipping), so you can get a hold of this if it sounds like something (and if you have an interest in the Incan empire, you should get a copy!) you want to check out.

Notes:

1. http://btripp-books.livejournal.com/106259.html

2-4. http://amzn.to/1RBNGU6

Monday, February 21, 2011[1]

Genesis, maybe ... Grail, not so much

This is an example of what happens sometimes when I get a book from one of those B&N clearance sales, where I'm shopping on price ($1.99) and volume (get 13 to make it over $25 for free shipping), and have to make do with the extremely brief descriptions that go along with those on-line listings. I had thought this book was going to be about "something completely different"! One would think a book titled Genesis of the Grail Kings[2] might have had something to do with Grail myths and European blood lines, yes? Yet Laurence Gardner's book never makes it past 1300 BCE ... which causes one to wonder where the "grail" bits come in.

I guess if one had been a *fan* of Mr. Gardner's (rather than having this particular book be one's introduction to his work), one would know that he has written a whole series of books which have various levels of connection to the "grail lineage". Of course, were one to have paid more attention to the sub-title: *"The Explosive Story of Genetic Cloning and the Ancient Bloodline of Jesus"* (even though there is only the most scant mention of that Jesus fellow in here), one might have figured that this was something else altogether. What "something else", you ask? Well, it turns out that most of this book is based on those pesky Anunnaki (Enlil, Enki, Marduk & company) which seem to have sprung full-formed out of the head of the recently deceased Zechariah Sitchin some decades back. I've read a half-dozen or so of Sitchin's books, so am reasonably familiar with the "mythos" involved, but if it's news to you, he was a researcher into Sumerian cuneiform writing who began to see a pattern in the materials he was handling which suggested an alternative translation from that which had been the "official line" ... this alternative involving *space aliens* who had come to earth and created modern man from existing hominid lines by way of splicing in their own DNA (now, doesn't that sub-title make a *lot* more sense?).

Like the poster said above Agent Mulder's desk, "I Want To Believe", but as enticing as the Sitchin version of history goes, it's all a bit sketchy and boils down to interpretations of quite ancient texts and images. Obviously, Gardner has bought this all "hook, line, & sinker", as it is the starting point for everything in this book. If he has solid ground to stand on, it's of the negative variety ... he's taking a look at timelines and lineages which *are not* Bible-based ... and, shockingly, to a large extent, the "official chronology" of middle-eastern archaeology is still very much fitted with "Bible blinders":

> "... the conventional chronology applied to the Egyptian dynasts in our history books was not compiled from Egyptian dates, but from the standard dating structure applied to the Old Testament. Archbishop Ussher of Armagh had published his

> biblical chronology in 1650, and the Egypt Exploration Fund was established in Victorian times with the express directive that archaeologists should seek to uphold the Old Testament tradition as dictated by the Christian Church."

Indeed, it appears that, until very recently, if research contradicted "Biblical" views, it would have a very hard time getting published, and, as Gardner points out, this was directly outlined for Egyptian research, and was at least tacitly in place for the much older (but, fortunately, more recently discovered) Sumerian material.

So, what is <u>Genesis of the Grail Kings</u>[3] about? Well ... it is, essentially, tracing the main characters of Genesis (up into Exodus) from their origins in the Sumerian (read: Anunnaki) culture, on into Egypt, and then back out of Egypt. Now, Gardner spins a very interesting tale here, but one has to, on one hand, be willing to grant him the whole "Anunnaki thing" on the front end, and then cut him a certain degree of slack on making connections between names and attributions across linguistic and cultural lines. Admittedly, Abraham was from Ur, and Ur was a major Sumerian city, but Gardner makes a whole net of connections of who the various begatters and begattees of biblical lineages came from and what they did. He especially wants to re-write traditional concepts about the Flood, Noah, and even Adam & Eve (who he attributes to being a "type" rather than specific individuals).

This all gets quite complicated ... with the struggle between Enlil and Enki effecting everything in Mesopotamia, and leading Abraham to move his family out of the region. This conflict carries on, as Enlil eventually is re-visioned as Jehovah, and there are differing traditions in the biblical narrative that come from the Enki/Anunnaki (multiple, married, mortal – if long-lived – deities) side of things, which get increasingly eradicated by the Enlil camp. Anyway, it turns out that Abraham and his family are "big deals" from Ur, and that there is a lot of Space Alien DNA in play with them. Eventually (you know the story: Abraham => Issac => Jacob => Joseph & brothers => Egypt) they end up in Egypt, and are not just "big wheels" in the court, but Gardner argues for assorted Biblical Patriarchs being actual historical Pharaohs.

Frankly, "the wheels came off the cart" to a large extent for me here. While Gardner had done a bit of linguistic stretching to get the early figures to match up with the right Sumerian locations, it was all "plausible" given the age and the sketchy info on both sides of the equation. However, with Egypt there is hundreds of years of research (albeit "Bible-biased") on the dynastic successions, etc., and the language links seem very thin (sort of like the folks who say that Nostradamus was writing about *Hitler* when his quatrain mentions "Hister", an old word for the Danube river). Here he tries to make a case that a major chunk of the late 18th Dynasty was, in fact, various biblical figures, with the most notable being Moses, who here becomes Akhenaten, with the worship of the Aten being the fore-runner of the Jehovian monotheism. Rather than being killed, he has Akhenaten being sent into exile, and eventually beginning the Sinai wanderings. While the

Aten-cult connection to the eventual Jewish religion has been posited (with varying degrees of plausibility) previously, there is little else here that is particularly convincing, just a barrage of names that have some slight arguable similarity, and small threads of context holding the argument together.

I don't even want to get into the details of the "white powder of gold" (which was a "food" for the Anunnaki and their descendants), but this figures in the story of Exodus and the place in the Sinai where Moses/Akhenaten "spoke to God" as being a "factory" for the stuff (*"not only is the powder of the highward fire-stone capable of raising human consciousness, but it is also a monatomic superconductor with no gravitational attraction"* ... I kid you not).

What is so frustrating with books like those of Sitchin and Gardner is that, on the whole, they're not "loopy" like some of the "newage" books I've reviewed here are ... they "look and feel" like solid pieces of serious research. Heck, this has something like 40 pages of notes, 40 pages of charts, diagrams, and other data, and a 16-page bibliography. But then you have Akhenaten/Moses taking the people of Israel to a Hathor temple in the middle of the Sinai to load up the Ark with a "monatomic superconductor" white powder to have for supplies on the road to the promised land. Very hard to buy into.

Anyway, once I got what the book was about, I did rather enjoy most of Genesis of the Grail Kings[4], as it was a jazz-like riff on some familiar, if "out there", theorizing. Needless to say, "your mileage may vary". If you want to dip a toe in this particular quagmire, you might do better with Sitchin's "Genesis Revisited", which at least spends more time making its arguments, but if this sort of thing "is your cup of tea", by all means go find a copy of this (the latest paperback edition is currently at 60% off at Amazon).

Notes:

1. http://btripp-books.livejournal.com/106744.html

2-4. http://amzn.to/1o9lj1T

Saturday, February 26, 2011[1]

What do YOU want?

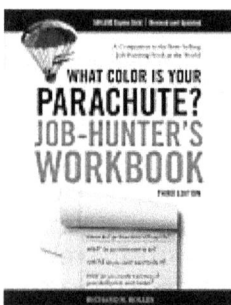

I know I've mentioned getting review copies of assorted books over the past year or so (this one courtesy of the fine folks at TenSpeed Press), but I wanted to note that it's never been a "firehose" of material, maybe one or two things a month, most of which just show up, unsolicited. Sometimes these grab me immediately and I'm eager to get into them, and other times, not so much. This is an example of one of the ones that ended up in the "whenever" pile, but came in handy.

The title of the moment is Richard N. Bolles' What Color Is Your Parachute? Job-Hunter's Workbook[2], a "companion piece" to his classic job-search book which is in its bazillionth edition at this point. I read that three or four job searches back and recalled that I was unthrilled with it at the time, being one of those guys who doesn't fit in the easy-to-define slots, and it seemed to me that books like WCIYP primarily exist to figure out what type of a gear you are so you can be in the right bin when a company comes looking for a very specific replacement part for their machine. Given my lack of enthusiasm for its "parent work", I didn't have particularly high expectations going into this, but I'd had another author ask me the favor of holding off reviewing his book until the week of its (still upcoming) release, so I was looking for something that I could quickly slot in to feature in my Monday The Job Stalker[3] blog post. I noticed that this was fairly short (all of 64 pages), and figured I could get it read and reviewed in plenty of time to make that switch.

Needless to say, this means that I haven't *done* any of the exercises outlined in What Color Is Your Parachute? Job-Hunter's Workbook[4], but I have given it a fair mental walk-through. To those familiar with the "technologies" of the job search, much of what Bolles pulls together here will be quite familiar, as, to a large extent this is simply assembling elements of various assessment devices and coordinating them into his "flower" model. This involves a graphic of 7 circles, a center one with six "petals" around it, each of these with information derived from a series of exercises.

The seven parts of the flower are Skills, Values/Goals/Purposes, Special Knowledges, People-Environments, Working Conditions, Level of Responsibility & Salary, and Geography. Each of these has its own section for determining what you "really want". The first, Skills, is probably the most involved, as he has readers write a series of *stories* of things they'd done in their lives which they enjoyed or had success at. Out of these one is to extract goals, obstacles, step-by-step activities, results, and any quantifiable/measurable data. Each of these stories is then analyzed according to a grid of specifics reflecting Physical Skills, Mental Skills, and Interpersonal Skills. These various assessments are then subjected to "prioritization grids" where everything is systematically subjected to A-B testing to determine a rank.

Similar exercises are given for the rest. Values takes your top 10 out of a list of 32 statements, and ends up determining your top 6 (I don't know about you, but *I* need more degrees of expression of values than is encompassed in 30-some prepackaged sentiments) which then go on the "flower". The "special knowledges" section has you list things "you know something about" sorted out by if you learned them in school, on the job, conferences and workshops, home study, or via volunteering and hobbies. This gets sorted via the same A-B testing grids, and then you're looking at "people" with a list of 24 activities that "you'd like to help people with" (again, this presupposes you *want* to help people, and are interested in any of Bolles' two dozen categories), this then also gets filtered into a prioritized list, before moving on to "things". This is the most out-of-touch part of this whole book, as it requires you to obtain *a phone book*, specifically *a yellow pages* (and he even says if you're planning on re-location to get one from your target area). I wonder what percentage of homes even *get* yellow pages these days? It's been *years* since we've had one actually at our door (there's a place in the service area in our building where one can grab one if so inclined), and it boggles the mind that a significant chunk of one of Bolles' steps here is based on finding one! Anyway, the third part of this is to go though the index of the yellow pages and highlight products or services that interest you. Once this is done, you take *this* list with the previous two, merge them together and do the A-B testing to come up with a list of the top *five* for that "petal".

The next "People-Environment" part is basically a way to come up with a Holland Code and Hexagon without actually taking the assessment … Bolles has a "party" exercise that he claims maps with a 93% accuracy to these results, and that's what your doing here, eventually filling in a Holland Hexagram with your top 3 of the Realistic, Investigative, Artistic, Social, Enterprising, and Conventional types.

For the "Working Conditions" petal of the flower, he has you list all the places you've worked, and noting what was "most distasteful" at each of those, ranking those, then turning each of those into a positive statement (i.e., "windowless cubicle" re-imaged as "office with a view"), and doing the A-B sorting on the positive list, the top five of which goes on the flower diagram.

The next one, Responsibility & Salary, is probably the biggest hassle, as Bolles asks the user to do a total financial analysis of their current condition to determine a "minimum" salary. I know there is no chance in Hell that *I'd* do that for this. Anyway, there's a brief assessment for responsibility level, the salary thing (a minimum and a "blue sky" target figure), and then a gesture towards "other rewards" (which I've seen done far more systematically in other books), in order to come up with four factors for the diagram. Finally, there's "Geography", with an assessment similar to that of the "Working Conditions" section, except that it has an extension to includes one's spouse/partner's data to come up with a consensus of 3 locations.

What are you supposed to do once you get Bolles' "Flower" filled out? Well, nothing really. You either get "a lightbulb moment" of clarity or you don't ... he has some coaching (on one page) on what to do in either of these cases, but it's not exactly *a plan*.

Again, I've processed *so much* of this sort of material over the various major job searches that I've been in over the past decade, that I have a hard time getting excited about anything in What Color Is Your Parachute? Job-Hunter's Workbook[5] ... to be honest, the most *useful* things for me to "take away" from this would be the prioritizing grids, as they present a solid system of figuring out one's preferences out of a wide field of options, which is certainly one of my main challenges.

This is brand new as of the end of 2010 (again, amazing it has that "yellow pages" thing in it!), so it should be available in book stores that carry job-search/career titles. It's not very expensive (as one would expect for a 64-pager), and Amazon has it for nearly half off, so this might be one of those to keep at the ready to push up a sub-$25 order into the free shipping zone. This is not a *bad* tool, and somebody coming new to the job search might well find its organization and compartmentalization of assessment elements a godsend, but in almost every aspect here it was "been there, done that" (heck, I was just looking at my Holland Hexagram this afternoon) for me.

Notes:

1. http://btripp-books.livejournal.com/107001.html
2. http://amzn.to/1Ro6GAb
3. http://jobstalker.info/
4-5. http://amzn.to/1Ro6GAb

Monday, February 28, 2011[1]

I must see this sometime ...

Yes, here is *another* of those charming little "Dover Thrift Editions" ... because, after all, anything that can turn a $23.98 book order (pending $7.56 in shipping charges) into a $25.48 order with *free* shipping, can be no *less* than charming, exhibiting as it does the effective aspect of *negative* cost! Given this magical quality, it really wouldn't matter too greatly *what* I added on to the order (although, I must admit, I spend way too much time poring over the seemingly *unending* options to find just the right one), but I've been making a solid effort to "kill two birds with one stone", as it were, and fill in holes in my literary education as well with these short, focused releases.

About half way through reading Oscar Wilde's The Importance of Being Earnest[2] I came to the rather shocking realization that I had, apparently, neither *read* nor *had seen* this previously. Obviously, as an English Major, I was *familiar* with the title, and the general concept that it was Wilde at his best, but it rang no bells. At this stage of my life, it should not come as such a surprise that I've "missed" key bits of the various areas I've studied, but I still feel somewhat abashed when something as "classic" as this managed to avoid me for all those decades. *And*, given what a delight this is, I feel a sense of loss in having not seen it performed in the many years that I was actively attending the Theater, as I'm sure that (in the right hands) this play would be quite a delight.

The Importance of Being Earnest[3] certainly owes a debt to the comedies of Shakespeare, as it has the same sort of mixed up relationships, secrets badly kept, timely entrances and exits, as in The Bard's comedic works. I wouldn't say this was *stolen* from any particular play (although my recall of the details of that portion of Shakespeare's works has faded over time), but the *ambiance* here clearly brings those to mind. The two main characters, a Mr. Jack Worthing, and a Mr. Algernon Moncrieff, are two young gentlemen seemingly of "the leisure class" (albeit one due to investments and one preferring to sponge off of family and friends over work) enjoying all the pleasures of Victorian-era London. Each of these fellows has been leading a "double life", one inventing a brother (Earnest) whose difficulties keep demanding Jack's presence in the capitol, and the other inventing an associate who is always in very ill health and requiring his (Algernon's) assistance. These fabrications allow them a freedom to follow their whims, but, ultimately, create a web of (comedic) complications. They both end up much enamored of a pair of young ladies, each who is connected to the other's family, and attempt to press engagements during the course of the play. Unfortunately, each has taken the identity of the fictitious Earnest to do so, and *both* of the young ladies are (somewhat inexplicably) much entranced with the name (to the extent that they completely dismiss the suitability of anybody by the *actual* names of the gentlemen).

Assorted additional characters take part in the confusion, as both fellows seek to be christened as "Earnest", and, as these things do, everything comes close to destruction before getting cleared up. If there was one part of this that I "had issues" with, it was how tidy the "tying up the loose ends" was ... as it turns out that what had seemed to have been a purely fictitious "tall tale" in the telling was the absolute truth of one of them, and that there was a very specific "importance" in "being Earnest".

What is also often charming in these Dover Thrift Editions is that they are frequently unabridged or even facsimile copies of much older books, in this case, it is a re-issue of an 1895 edition of the play, complete with information on the theater at which it was being staged, *and* the long-dead actors playing the parts. This sort of "window back in time" is always a nice bonus in these volumes.

This edition of <u>The Importance of Being Earnest</u>[4] is quite current, however, and is available. Unfortunately, the odds are (as I've noted before) unlikely that a "brick & mortar" vendor will stock it, as the retail mark-up on a book bearing a $1.50 cover price is not likely to support even the scant shelf space it would require. Which brings me back to the first point above ... stash it on your on-line vendor's "wish list" and have it ready to go the next time you find yourself ordering a couple of $11.99 books and need something to nudge that up into the free shipping promised land.

Notes:

1. http://btripp-books.livejournal.com/107058.html

2-4. http://amzn.to/1Ro3vZn

Saturday, March 5, 2011[1]

Pointing ahead ...

I spent ten years running my own publishing company back in the 90's, so I've lived the small dramas that are always involved with the process of books being born. One of the more obscure pleasures of Twitter has been to voyeuristically experience this process again as several folks I follow have steered various books into the light. Oddly, it's with the authors "I know" (unfortunately, generally just in a "pixel people" context, although I've had the pleasure of meeting a few IRL) that I have to go hitting up the publishers for review copies. Fortunately, the folks at Harper Business were happy to send along this well in advance of its release date.

Gary Vaynerchuk has been an icon in the social media sphere, especially for his use of web video to build a business (he grew his family's liquor store business into a $60million/year juggernaut in just a few years). Gary's previous book Crush It![2] was a formative philosophical document of the current social media sphere, and his latest, The Thank You Economy[3] takes a further look at how business is having to change to survive in a constantly-connected world.

While the book has structure (it's in five parts, Welcome to the TYE, How to Win, The TYE in Action, Sawdust [a collection of bits and pieces], and a 2-page "quick version" at the end), it's not particularly *linear*, but runs through thoughts, rants, examples, and overviews of trends. One section, however, has enough structure to discuss independently, and that's Chapter Three: Why Smart People Dismiss Social Media, and Why They Shouldn't, where the author reflects on the consulting he's done with large companies, and the sort of fear-based justifications that he's heard, with a list of eleven of these, and "answers" for each:

1. There's no ROI.
2. The metrics aren't reliable.
3. Social media is still too young.
4. Social Media is just another trend that will pass.
5. We need to control our message
6. I don't have time to keep track of what every Joe or Jane says, and I can't afford/don't want to pay someone else to do it.
7. We're doing fine without it.
8. We tried it; it doesn't work.
9. The legal issues are too thorny.

10. *It takes too long to pay off.*

11. *Social media works only for startup, life-style, or tech brands.*

In each case, Vaynerchuk says "The Answer Is Always The Same":

> *I think we're entering a business golden age. It took a long time for people to recognize the value of intellectual capital, whose intangible assets don't show up on a spreadsheet, couldn't be tracked, and couldn't be expressed in dollars. Now it's widely understood that intellectual capital is part of the backbone of every organization, and worth protecting. While the ability to form relationships has always been considered a subset of intellectual capital, social media has catapulted that skill into a wealth-building category. In the future, the companies with tremendous "relationship capital" will be the ones to succeed.*

How does a company succeed in the new reality? By *caring*, and the ones that "out-care" their competitors are the one that will come out on top. The author suggests that we're returning to "small town" realities, made possible by the immediacy and intimacy of social media's capabilities to allow person-to-person communications on the Web.

> *These decades that brought greater distance between friends, family, and neighbors coincided with the rapid rise of big business. … Eventually {the corporation's} reason for being less about {its core business activities} or building a legacy, and more about satisfying quarterly returns and improving stock options. The prioritization of profit over principle quickly took over American corporate culture and is what shaped the perspective of all ranks of many of today's business leaders. Most have never known anything else. They're just playing the game as they were taught.*
>
> …
>
> *Anyone waiting for the marketing landscape to stabilize before incorporating social media into his or her business strategy is living in a fantasy world. We're riding a really, really fast train; the changes we've seen mark only the beginning of the transformations yet to come. Stable isn't going to happen any time soon.*
>
> …
>
> *Social media gives us the opportunity to figure out what people want before they even know that they want it. Using social media to talk to customers is like getting access to the most honest focus group that's ever sat around a conference table … We have to listen, participate in the conversation, ask questions, and solicit feedback. We have to be more involved, and more attentive, and more interested, than we have ever been.*

Again, one of the things which gives Vaynerchuk "gravitas" in these arguments is that *he's done it*, he's taken his gospel of social media and in a short period of time taken a business to a level *fifteen times* what they'd started at when he began implementing these ideas. This is not "ivory tower" philosophizing, but the words of a guy who's been hustling in the trenches, and creating a huge success story for himself.

The Thank You Economy[4] is filled with theory, practical advice, and detailed looks at how numerous companies have used social media successfully, and some who have dropped the ball. He takes particular looks at how companies like Zappos have made solid connections with their staff and customers to create a culture that is far richer (and profitable) than most "conventional" models. He also picks apart several social media programs (that you would recognize) showing how they worked, didn't work, or could have worked better. There are also profiles of a wide range of *types* of business here, and how the particular challenges of each benefited by moving into the TYE model.

Of particular interest to me were some nuggets from the author's research ... one particularly stood out as "context" for the communication-rich environment we're in: *"Just how much information are we trying to absorb? At the 2010 Techonomy conference in Lake Tahoe, California, Google CEO Eric Schmidt stated that every two days people create as much information at they did from the dawn of civilization to 2003, about five exabytes of data."*... that's amazing!!!

While this is a book primarily for businesses, it's a wake-up call for everybody on the changing *nature* of business, as society becomes more and more intertwined with its communication systems. Approaches which were solid and time-tested a decade ago are suddenly approaching the point of being useless, and whole industries may go the way of sheet music and sealing wax in the near future. For the job seeker (or worker looking to *keep* their job), this is a look into what sorts of skill sets are likely to be in demand on-going ... and I highly recommend it to all and sundry on this basis.

As I'm writing this, The Thank You Economy[5] is just shipping, so it will likely be in your larger brick-and-mortar book vendors in days. However, both Amazon and BN.com have it for pre-order at nearly half off the cover price, enabling you to pick it up with another book (perhaps Vaynerchuk's previous title Crush It![6]?) for just a smidge over the $25 free-shipping line!

Notes:

1. http://btripp-books.livejournal.com/107420.html

2. http://btripp-books.livejournal.com/88717.html

3-5. http://amzn.to/1pApXXS

6. http://btripp-books.livejournal.com/88717.html

Sunday, March 6, 2011[1]

Foreshadowing "Social Media" ...

One of the occasional joys of getting nearly "random" books from things like the B&N.com clearance sales (where descriptions of the books are tweet-like in their minimalism) is encountering "a gem" that would have never come to my attention if it wasn't sitting there for $1.99 ... I typically will scour those listings to find 13 "likely" books to order, to get a total over the free shipping line, and will frequently end up adding things just because they "sound interesting". Harry Beckwith's The Invisible Touch: The Four Keys to Modern Marketing[2] was one of these.

This is not a "new" book, having come out in 2000, so it can't really be considered a "social media" book (as that moniker had only just been coined around then), but it could certainly be described as an "Ur-SocialMedia" book, as much of what Beckwith discusses here could as easily have flowed from the keyboards of Brogan, Vaynerchuk, or Stratten a decade later. The perceptions here, like those in some of Seth Godin's early books, seem remarkably visionary, if having details that are almost "quaintly" off-base (in a discussion of branding he looks at search engines and notes that 3/4ths of respondents say they used Yahoo! vs. Excite, Dogpile, AlteVista, or Northern Light ... a little company called "Google" was obviously not even on his radar at that point!).

The book is really in two parts, a first almost "philosophical" portion, taking up a third of the book, and then the sub-title's "four keys". To me, the "meat" here is in that first part, as this is where he sets the stage for the rest, and quite accurately details many trends which are blossoming in the present time. This part consists of three sections, "Research and Its Limits", "Fallacies of Marketing", and "What Is Satisfaction?", each contemplating the realities of these business elements ... some quotes:

> If people sought only basic services, Caribou's double cappuccinos would cost less than Taco Bell's burritos, because the raw ingredients and labor cost less. Consumers buy more than things; they purchase connections. ... Our lives seem increasingly disconnected ... technology reduces direct contact with people. Our drive for connection grows more intense. Making genuine, human connections become more important everywhere – not least of all in our business every day.
>
> ...
>
> People who know they are being studied change what they do. ... Research changes its own results ... if a researcher can effect the relationships among protons and neutrons, what does this tell us about the validity of research into people's attitudes and behaviors?
>
> ...

> *The more innovative your idea, the smaller the number of people who will understand it – and people have great trouble imagining that they will buy something they cannot understand. … The more innovative the idea, the less likely it is to survive this kind {opinion surveys, etc.} of scrutiny. And yet the more innovative the idea, the greater the potential success. Research supports mediocre ideas and kills great ones.*
>
> *…*
>
> *We limit ourselves if we fail to recognize not just the extraordinary marketing power in being known to a prospective buyer, but the liability in being little known – or not known at all. … Deep in our genetic code, an instruction warns us to treat the unfamiliar with suspicion. The Unfamiliar is a threat we must avoid or overcome. … unfamiliarity breeds more than indifference. It breeds contempt.*
>
> *…*
>
> *We experience what we believe we will experience. This means that anything and everything a service can do to convey quality, expertise, and the ability to perform well likely will enhance client satisfaction. Conveying quality can be as critical to satisfaction as actually delivering quality.*

The rest of the book looks at what Beckwith defines as "the four keys", which are Price, Brand, Packaging, and Relationships. Each factor he looks at here is generally a counter-intuitive revelation about marketing a product or service. Each sub-section within these "keys" also closes with a take-away sentence reflecting the essence of that point. The author looks at companies, industries, different sorts of businesses, and how they exemplify these concepts. Like in the first part of the book, much of this deals with human psychology, and there are certainly eye-openers in here. If there was one particular "disappointment" I had with the book it's that there are no references or foot/end notes to point to specific bits of research. This makes one feel that much of this is "shot from the hip", and that one has to take his word for it all.

Given that one caveat, I was quite enthusiastic with The Invisible Touch[3], and found the vast majority of what Beckwith presents here both prescient and profoundly perceptive. I have not only *recommended* this to various associates, but have even *ordered copies* for a couple of folks I'm doing consulting projects with. The hardcover edition I have seems to be out of print (although available used for as little as 1¢) but there's a paperback edition that's available, plus versions for the Kindle and Nook. If you have an interest in marketing, it's something you should definitely pick up!

Notes:

1. http://btripp-books.livejournal.com/107638.html

2-3. http://amzn.to/1Ro1lsH

Saturday, March 12, 2011[1]

Quite a find ...

I probably mentioned the Open Books[2] box sale at some point, and here comes the first of the many books picked up there. For a long time I had avoided buying used books because I didn't like the sense that I had "obtained some dead person's property", but over long spans of unemployment I "got over it", to a large extent. This is very likely a book in that category, being a 1959 edition with a gift inscription (with a quote from Dag Hammarskjöld) up front from December of 1968 ... forty-two years ago.

This copy of Zen Buddhism, An Introduction to Zen with Stories, Parables and Koan Riddles of the Zen Masters, Decorated with Figures from Old Chinese Ink-Paintings[3] is in really remarkable condition, given its vintage (a 1959 hardcover), with just minor tearing to its dust jacket. It is a very attractive volume, nicely designed and laid out, but odd in having no author/editor attribution and very little publishing info (this was before the SBN code was introduced, let alone the ISBN), with most sources simply identifying this as being from Peter Pauper Press. I'd encountered books from them before, and they tended towards beautiful, uncluttered design, with straight-forward presentations, and this is no exception to that.

At 60 pages, Zen Buddhism[4] is hardly an in-depth look at the subject, but is "a tasting menu" of many of the attributes of Zen, which could serve as a delightful introduction to somebody newly coming to the subject, or a very pleasant indulgence for those familiar with the literature. I've read many Zen books over the years, and this was certainly an enjoyable way to fill up a couple of bus rides!

> Shuzan held up his staff and waved it before his monks.
>
> "If you call this a staff," he said, "you deny its eternal life.
>
> If you do not call this a staff, you deny its present fact.
>
> Tell me just what do you propose to call it?"

The selections here range from the very brief excerpts such as the above to a 7-page introductory essay, with various items, from multi-page transmission tales to famous Koans, in between. What comes through here is something of the *essence* of Zen, in a very attractive and non-doctrinal package.

Somewhat remarkably, a half a century past its publication, one can find numerous copies of Peter Pauper Press' Zen Buddhism[5] in the used listings, at various prices and in assorted conditions. Unfortunately, lacking an ISBN or other identifier, it is somewhat hit-or-miss, with several nearly-identical entries (some with as many as 14 copies available) out there. I am happy to now have a copy of this (although wonder at its history), and I suspect that most of my readers would too, so if you're interested, it's worth some searching to find the right one for you.

Notes:

1. http://btripp-books.livejournal.com/107989.html
2. http://www.open-books.org/
3-5. http://amzn.to/1Ro0pV9

Sunday, March 13, 2011[1]

In search of the remarkable ...

Here's another gem picked up at the Open Books[2] box sale last weekend. As regular readers of this space have no doubt figured out, I've become something of a fan of Seth Godin, having come into possession of several of his books from various sources over the past year or so, and I was very pleased to find a copy of his Purple Cow: Transform Your Business by Being Remarkable[3].

One of the problems, I suppose, of being "a visionary" is that one is, somewhat by definition, required to be looking forward into a hazy future without anything *near* omniscience, and so, as they age, one's books acquire anachronisms of focusing on things that didn't quite work out the way it seemed they might when ink hit the page. Purple Cow[4] came out in 2003, and while this is hardly *antique*, those 8 years are a *very long time* in the tech sphere. In this case the "whopper" came in a case study of Motorola and Nokia, where Godin seems to be writing off the cell phone market (he says *"The sad truth, though, is that ... the Purple Cow has left the room and there's not a lot the cell phone companies can do about it."*, despite both companies *"scrambling to market phones that send photographs"*) ... I guess the Cow came back for an encore in that niche four years later when Apple introduced the iPhone!

The thrust of the book, however, is really more about a change in modalities across the entire spectrum of business, moving from what he describes as "The TV-Industrial Complex" into a "Post-TV Age", where the classic model of buying vast amounts of advertising and having that drive sales is just not working like it used to. He uses a bell-curve illustration to break out sections of the market, from "innovators" on the very leading edge, to the "early adopters", on into the "early and late majority", and finally into the "laggards".

> The marketer of yesterday valued the volume of people she could reach. ... Mass marketing traditionally targets the early and late majority because this is the largest group. But in many markets, the **value** of a group isn't related to its size – a group's value is related to its influence. In this market, for example, the early adopters heavily influence the rest of the curve, so persuading them is worth far more than wasting ad dollars trying to persuade anyone else.

At this point Godin brings in the concept of an "ideavirus" and the "Sneezers" who spread it.

> Every market has a few sneezers. They're often the early adopters, but not always. Finding and seduc-

> ing these sneezers is the essential step in creating an ideavirus.

Godin says that targeting a particular niche allows you to effectively get to the "sneezers" that would be too difficult to find in mass-market products. And, finding a "Purple Cow" gets these key voices on board. However, it's not always easy to implement this ...

> The Problem with the Cow
>
> ... is actually the problem with fear.
>
> If being a Purple Cow is such an easy, effective way to break through the clutter, why doesn't everyone do it? Why is it so hard to be Purple?
>
> Some folks would like you to believe that there are too few great ideas or that their product or their industry or their company can't support a great idea. This, of course, is nonsense.
>
> The Cow is so rare because people are afraid.
>
> If you're remarkable, it's likely that some people won't like you. That's part of the definition of remarkable. Nobody gets unanimous praise – ever. The best the timid can hope for is to be unnoticed. Criticism comes to those who stand out.

Much of the book is spent with examples, considerations, and case studies, most ending with a very focused "take-away point" ... although he certainly fleshes the concepts raised here out much more in his later book Free Prize Inside[5]. More info (including later "bonus chapters") can be found at http://apurplecow.com[6]

Purple Cow[7] is still in print (in a later, updated edition), and both Amazon and B&N have it for about 1/3rd off of cover, but you can also find "very good" copies of the 2003 hardcover (that I have) for under a buck via the new/used vendors. If this is the sort of thing which is of interest to you, I'd definitely recommend picking up a copy.

Notes:

1. http://btripp-books.livejournal.com/108106.html
2. http://www.open-books.org/
3-4. http://amzn.to/1XQmaRb
5. http://btripp-books.livejournal.com/99621.html
6. http://apurplecow.com/
7. http://amzn.to/1XQmaRb

Sunday, March 20, 2011[1]

Valuable but frustrating ...

This was one of those books that has come to me via the LibraryThing.com "Early Reviewers" program ... it *would* have been an "early" review had the book come out on time, but this was from the *December* batch (with a February 15 release date) and only arrived this week. I suppose the benefit (for me) of the delay was that, instead of getting an ARC (advance reader copy, often in various degrees of not being "finished"), they ended up sending out the hardcover. I was initially somewhat surprised to have been selected to get James Redfield's The Twelfth Insight: The Hour of Decision[2] as I was under the impression that I'd "lost touch" with the Celestine material after reading his early books "back in the day". However, I recently discovered that his books on the tenth and eleventh "insights" (which I've read) were *not*, as I had supposed, preceded by separate volumes on the first through the ninth, so I guess I'm pretty much "up to speed" on his stuff.

Of course, "up to speed" is hardly "on the bandwagon", as anybody who read my review of The Secret of Shambhala: In Search of the Eleventh Insight[3] will recall. I had attributed my "issues" with that largely to my not reading much fiction, but early on in this one I realized that it was not so much it being fiction, as it being extremely *flat* fiction. As opposed to even other books more-or-less in this genre (such as the Castaneda corpus), there is almost *no* descriptive copy about people, places, and things, and the resulting effect is like watching a stick-figure animation as opposed to an actual movie. It almost feels like he'll look up a handful of attributes about a region, and then drop them in, where one might expect more scene-setting. Again, it's like stick figures walking through a stick-figure scene with an occasional *label* on something (like mentioning a place had cottonwood trees, or that a house was adobe) and letting it stand with that.

Most of the text is the inner discourse of the unnamed protagonist, interspersed with wooden dialog, and the occasional oration where one of the characters will launch into a spiel on some subject that Redfield is obviously wanting to get around to. As I've previously noted, the sense that the author has never *seen* the places he's writing about, let alone *been* there, is a constant in these books, and this may be more from this "symbolic" (it is a red mountain, very much like the other red mountain) style than the author's total disconnect from the particulars that has been *my* take-away when reading these. Of course, who am I to judge a guy who's created an entire publishing *empire* for himself cranking out books in this particular voice? Again, this is one of the main reasons why "I quit reading fiction", as I'd prefer my metaphysics come to me in a treatise than in a fable.

This all being said ... I found The Twelfth Insight[4] a remarkable read. As I've discussed in the context of his other books, Redfield is aggravating in that there are gems of *really* powerful spiritual perceptions and/or techniques buried in the two-dimensional mud of the narrative. Usually, there will be a scant handful of points in his writing where I'm sticking in a bookmark and getting excited mentally cross-referencing what he's presented with other related concepts, traditions, and practices from my own studies. Well, in this one, they just keep on coming, and for a book which I had very low expectations, I was engaged and eager to press on to the next part.

This is likely due to the (predictably sketchy) over-arching concept here that some poorly-defined group of mysterious people were responsible for "the secret release of an old, unnamed Document" which had "both Hebrew and Arabic origins" ... this only appears in translation (from what? by whom?) with no indication of its origins (as opposed to a Dead Sea Scrolls sort of "fragmentary" state, this appears to be one complete document, the parts of which are "appearing" ... in xerox copies of translations ... in various places around the globe). There are twelve "Integrations" which are detailed in the bits and pieces that conveniently pop up as needed. As weak as this structure is, each of the elements have those little bits of "shiny" truth buried in the text, and so it draws one into the clumsy narrative despite the stick-figure dynamics.

The main plot is that these sections of this "Document" start appearing, and the protagonist and his associate Wil jet off to find out more about these. The initial part of the book involves them heading off to Sedona, where Wil's Hopi friends inexplicably tie this in to the Mayan Calendar (the whole "2012" thing hangs over this, and it is set in "Spring of 2011"). It would have been *much* more interesting to have woven in the Hopi prophesies and world vision here, but I guess it's far more *marketable* to hook onto the hot apocalypse of the moment. Eventually, the group he's working with jets off for Egypt and beyond (there never is much attention paid to who's funding these trips), to head for the area around Mt. Sinai. Opposing "the good guys" are a global conspiracy of primarily Islamic and Evangelical "Apocalyptics" who have teamed up to try to start a global nuclear war, and bring on whatever version of end-time end-games happens to play out. It is an interesting perspective that these folks are *deeply* disturbed by all new age and/or "human development" teaching and are pretty much "over the edge" looking to protect their own mythos, enough so that they're willing to conspire with equally-unhinged extremists of "enemy" groups to trigger Armageddon.

Of course, the protagonist (who is, really, *very* "clueless" most of the time ... I found myself mentally yelling at him about stuff that he learned, but wasn't using, from the *last* book!) and his band find the right parts of the Document at the right times and are able to rapidly advance through the assorted "Integrations" to the point where they're able to save the day. But you expected that, right? Again, this is a disappointingly *written* book which still harbors in it sufficiently high-quality spiritual material that I feel that I have to recommend it. Go figure. I would have *loved* for Redfield to have actually *provided* "the Document", but there aren't even scraps to piece together, just people talking about it ... however, if any of what he's "hidden in the text" is actually *true* (and, especially, is hooked into a 2012 schedule), this is something that anybody with a metaphysical bent might want to have read.

As The Twelfth Insight[5] is brand-new (it's still just out in Hardcover and grossly-overpriced electronic editions), you're likely to have to find it at retail. Fortunately, both Amazon and B&N have it at more than 40% off online, which would be your best bet at the moment.

Notes:

1. http://btripp-books.livejournal.com/108371.html

2. http://amzn.to/1o94pjU

3. http://btripp-books.livejournal.com/99998.html

4-5. http://amzn.to/1o94pjU

Monday, March 21, 2011[1]

Not for everybody ...

I ended up getting this book as part of a "package deal" at a networking event where one of the authors was speaking ... I'm not so sure that I would have picked it up otherwise. While it *is* a "social media" book, this is far more than most aimed at "companies" rather than to individuals, and is very "strategic" in that context. If I was still the Director of Communications of some company (and wasn't already enmeshed in social media), this is the sort of book that I'd want to have handed to me. Unfortunately, I'm approaching *two years* out of work, and not only do I not *have* a company for which to implement something like this, I also don't have the nice "extras" like a smart phone and a data plan. I bring up this point because the book has a couple of dozen "extras" which are available only via Microsoft Tags, which are sort of like QR codes, but Microsoft's proprietary system. I was *amazed* that there wasn't any alternative approach for connecting to this material other than via one's smart phone ... I can't be the *only* person out there without a one (although, I must admit, that at most networking events I attend it sometimes seems that way). Would it have *killed* them to have done a bit.ly link to put in the description copy that accompanied each of the MS Tags? I don't think so. It just so happens that I "know" both of the authors from Twitter, and have been nagging them about this point ... unfortunately, neither of the web sites noted in the book have any clear way of finding the info (although a list of links *is* on one page on one of the sites, it doesn't appear to be linked *to* from anywhere else, and, on top of that, several of the links are already broken). Needless to say, having developed web sites and promotional programs (i.e. exactly this kind of thing) for many years, this drove me nuts.

Anyway ...

The NOW Revolution: 7 Shifts to Make Your Business Faster, Smarter and More Social[2] is a cooperative effort of Amber Naslund (@AmberCadabra[3]), VP of Social Strategy for social monitoring service Radian6, and Jay Baer (@JayBaer[4]), Social Media Strategy Consultant and founder of Convince & Convert. They both bring a lot of business acumen to the table here, and have put together a book which is targeted differently from most of those that I've covered in this space. Personally, I don't get the concept of "7 Shifts" particularly ... yes, these are seven areas that will need to be addressed for most companies to implement effective social media interfaces, but each is, generally speaking, too broad to efficiently be addressed as a particular "shift" ... but that might just be me.

Again, this is very much targeted to those at a company/corporation who have been tasked with "doing some of this social media stuff", and is, on one hand, somewhat targeted to the social media "newbie", but is, on the other hand, very much addressing somebody solidly ensconced in the corporate structure. It took me a good quarter of the book to really "get in sync" with it, as it initially just read "flat" (certainly as compared to other social media books out there like Scott Stratten's Unmarketing[5]!), but once I "got" that this was more of the "internal memo" sort of business document its tone started to fit. This sort of takes the thrust of David Meerman Scott's Real-Time Marketing and PR[6] and pieces together a step-by-step outline for how a company might expand into the social media sphere.

The "7 Shifts" here are as follows:

1. Engineer a New Bedrock

   This looks at the "culture" of the company/organization. To effectively use social media, there needs to have "speed, nimbleness, and decentralized decision making", while embracing independence and a free flow of ideas. Sadly, this is likely the biggest hurdle for most companies, as its not only involves the commitment of those at the top, but a level open communications far beyond the present norm.

2. Find Talent You Can Trust

   Needless to say, to achieve the aims here requires a different sort of employee with a different collection of skills. Frankly, I found this section encouraging, as the ideal hire in this scenario is the "well rounded" sort, which is a 180° turn-about from the "precise parallelogram" peg/hole model so prevalent in the current job market!

3. Organize Your Armies

   Developing a "real-time" business will demand organizational models that "will distribute decision making and authority throughout the company" with "faster, more fluid communications within and among the ranks".

4. Answer the New Telephone

   "Just like you've put a phone on everyone's desk in your company, you'll incorporate social media listening capabilities into your work to power your day-to-day business." This won't all happen at once, but will move from implementing a few tools to the point of total involvement.

5. Emphasize Response-Ability

   Two concepts here, the "Humanization Highway" of ever-increasing engagement, and the "Opportunity Economy" which allows your products and services to be "pulled" by the customer. "You'll start talking to your customers in ways you never have before ... what starts as reacting and responding will give way to contribution and participation, even your own storytelling."

6. Build a Fire Extinguisher

    Obviously, one of the essential roles for Social Media is "putting out fires" when they arise. This "shift" deals with creating response plans which empower employees to be a the point of crisis response, with clear structures of how communication flows in crisis.

7. Make a Calculator

    Sure, everybody wants to know what's the ROI on social media ... here's how to determine your organization's Key Performance Indicators, and measure how the metrics work for these.

An interesting bit of data from this last section is how many results Google comes up with for "social media ROI" verses ROI for any other advertising medium, 208,000 for social media, with the next highest being "e-mail ROI" at 12,200 ... and "billboard ROI" squeaking in at a mere *148* ... obviously the quip "what's the ROI on the telephone?" hasn't quite filtered into the zeitgeist, as most folks are still trying to wrest "exact numbers" for social media, while plainly "vague" numbers (entire markets generalized from samples only a fraction of a percent of the population) are common currency in most other vehicles!

It's certain that eventually Social Media will become as much a necessary tool as any of the standard "commercial message" vehicles have been, and the movement in this direction will change almost everything about business. The NOW Revolution[7] is a handbook on how to bring one's company into that new reality sooner rather than later. As this has only been out for a month or so at this point, it's probably both available at the brick-and-mortar book vendors with business sections, and at the best discount from Amazon and B&N on-line. If you're involved in social media, you will probably want to add this to your knowledge bank, and if you're in a position with a company that's seeing the writing on the wall about *needing* a social media program, this is certainly something you'll want to pick up.

Notes:

1. http://btripp-books.livejournal.com/108780.html
2. http://amzn.to/1Lz3qPH
3. https://twitter.com/AmberCadabra
4. https://twitter.com/jaybaer
5. http://btripp-books.livejournal.com/101421.html
6. http://btripp-books.livejournal.com/105905.html
7. http://amzn.to/1Lz3qPH

Saturday, March 26, 2011[1]

Be werry werry kwiet ...

This is another of those "dollar store finds", and had been sitting around for quite a while waiting for me to be in the right mood for a book on fighting terrorism. As I'd plowed through so many "social media" and similar things of late, I figured that this would be something to throw into the mix to shake stuff loose a bit. Like many of the books I've picked up for a buck, this one soon showed why it was kicking around in that channel!

On the Hunt: How to Wake Up Washington and Win the War on Terror[2] is by frequent Fox News contributor Col. David Hunt, who (if I recall correctly) was one of the go-to guys in coverage on the second Gulf War. He has "has over 29 years of military experience including extensive operational experience in special operations, counter terrorism and intelligence operations" and is rather impassioned on the subject of military virtues.

"Passion" probably doesn't go far enough when describing the tone of this book, Hunt is hopping mad, and obviously deeply frustrated with how the "war on terror" is going ... and it's quite a revelation when one realizes that this was written in 2007, so the railing he's doing here *was at the Bush administration* ... I can just imagine how close to "busting a blood vessel" he's been since the ascension of Kommissar Zero to the Presidency!

The book is about 2/3 text and 1/3 assorted supporting materials. I wish that there was more *organization* to that appendix section, as some of it is quite fascinating (Al Qaeda training materials for *their* snipers, instructions for making quick-change license plates, information on the Iran-supplied roadside bombs, etc.) but it's pretty much just dumped in there with no specific explanatory copy, along with assorted reports, white papers, and what appear to be PowerPoint slides.

Frankly, I think they should have used one of the chapter headings for the title of this book, as it would have conveyed the "feel" of it better: *Bravest of the Brave, Led by Idiots* ... this is pretty much the thrust here. Hunt keeps outlining how the politicians and career "desk" military men constantly screw things up. One of the more "titillating" things here is that Hunt "names names" and is happy to tell you just what jerks, idiots, and brown-nosers certain well-known names from the news are. I found it especially fascinating how much he *hates* Donald Rumsfeld (whom I always had found appealing for the way he treated the White House press corps like a troop of feces-flinging monkeys) ... and he doesn't have much more love for most of that administration.

Now, lest one think that Hunt's some sort of Wesley Clark leftist (although, I have to admit, some of Hunt's ranting came close to what you'd expect from that side of the barricades!), he's obviously *not*, but was bordering on being unhinged by how ineffectual the Bush administration was in fighting terror and securing our borders. Let me give you a sample of a typical part of this:

> *Actually, there are bigger questions: If we know all this about the terrorists, their capabilities, and their intentions, why don't we respond appropriately? Why have we allowed the war to become politicized, when real leaders would be focused on the task at hand – killing the bad guys?*
>
> *Unfortunately, our leadership in this war has not stepped up to the challenge. In Iraq, a Navy SEAL element, a Special Forces company, or a Delta Force squadron could open up the airport road in less than a month; they could clear an entire town the size of Basra and maintain the peace with their Iraqi counterparts there in six months; they could stop infiltrators along a section of border immediately. They could do magic if only they were allowed to do their jobs. So, how in hell was an entire Navy SEAL element allowed to sit on their powerful, perfectly trained asses for an entire year? They did next to nothing – even though they begged for a mission and are the best in the world at what they do. They sat on their asses because their leaders and their leaders' leaders are risk-averse, PowerPoint-briefing, politically correct, do-nothing assholes. The SEAL element actually gained weight on a deployment when they usually lose ten pounds per man.*
>
> *This is wrong; this is how we lose. This is how an insurgency grows and a civil war materializes.*

Just in case Col. Hunt isn't making himself clear, he later goes over, name by name, most of the desk-sitters responsible for running the Iraq campaign and wraps up with:

> *These are not officers; these are not leaders; these are cowards, faux officers, play soldiers, and poor excuses for leaders. Never has this nation, this military, been witness to such low-life, scum-sucking, bottom-feeders as this crew.*

Needless to say, there's a certain "make the popcorn" aspect to reading this stuff and seeing who's next in Hunt's cross-hairs … if only the nature of the problems weren't so damn serious! I do, however, hope that the V.A. is supplying the Colonel with some good drugs to keep his blood pressure down and his mood stabilized these days, because, again, all the above *sturm und drang* is focused on the *Bush* administration, which was lightyears ahead of the current mob at the White House in terms of addressing Iraq/Afghanistan, the Border, and containment of the terror threat in general.

As noted, I found On the Hunt[3] at the dollar store, but I see that Amazon, at least, is still selling it at retail, so I guess it's not "out of print" per se. If this sounds like a fun read to you, you'll probably want to go check out the new/used vendors who have copies of the hardcover in "very good" condition for a penny and "new" for under fifty cents!

Notes:

1. http://btripp-books.livejournal.com/109026.html
2-3. http://amzn.to/1UODt5W

Sunday, March 27, 2011[1]

Hey, I'd settle for ONE!

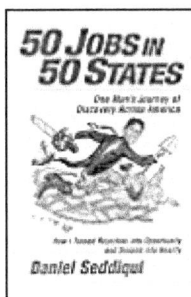

Since I've been writing my _The Job Stalker_[2] blog over on the Tribune's "ChicagoNow" site, and featuring reviews from here, I've begun to have several publishers keeping me at least on their query list for new titles in the "jobs" area. This one is courtesy Berrett-Koehler ... and is something of a doozy, being the adventures of one guy who got it in his head to work in each of the 50 states (for at least a few days) in some job that he felt typified that state.

Daniel Seddiqui had graduated from USC in 2005 with a degree in economics, and had set out to get a job in his field. Forty non-productive job interviews (and how I envy him getting that many interviews!) later, he was still not employed and was losing the support of his parents (one of the more poignant bits here, from one long-term-unemployed person to another, was how his family was seemingly unsympathetic to the lack of success in his job search ... it really sucks to be putting in 12-18 hours a day _trying_ to find a job, and be treated like you're lounging on the couch popping bon-bons). On top of this, he was having difficulties with a long-distance relationship, and so was in a rather bad place.

Somewhere in these struggles the idea popped into his head to go find a job in each state of the country that would be representative of that state. If there was one "cognitive disconnect" for me in the book, it's how he went from not even being able to land a _dishwasher_ job back home to venturing off to find _fifty_ jobs in locales he'd never been. I guess this is a testimony to the place he was mentally at that point, with the project being a desperate lurch "out of the box". This eventually became 50 Jobs in 50 States: One Man's Journey of Discovery Across America[3] which chronicles his 2009 journey across the country.

Seddiqui appears to be a rather persistent fellow, having, for almost every job, done massive campaigns to find _somebody_ in a particular industry in each state who would hire him. Again, I still have a hard time imagining reaching out to this many people to just get a temp job for a week, but that is evidently what he did to make this work. He did set up a blog to track his progress, and was media savvy enough to make himself available to local press, but it took getting the attention of some _Asian_ TV crews to start building a buzz, and once that started, some folks evidently hired him to be an "attraction".

While he did not "jump around" too much, he also didn't exactly take the most direct route to many states. The book is broken up into medium-sized sections of 3-7 states each, following as he moves around the country. He obtained a used jeep to serve as his main source of transportation, and in several cases, this served as his lodging as well. Anyway, to get a sense of what he got into in his year on the road, here's the list of state, city, occupation and employer for each:

> Utah: Salt Lake City - "Humanitarian Services" with the Mormons; Colorado: Denver - "Hydrologist" with the United States Geological Survey; South Dakota: Sioux Falls - "Rodeo Announcer" with the South Dakota Rodeo Association; North Dakota: Fargo - "Engineer Cartographer" with the Ulteig company; Minnesota: Elk River - "Medical Device Machinist" with Metal Craft Medical Manufacturing; Iowa: Ames - "Agronomist" with Iowa State University; Nebraska: Lincoln - "Corn Farmer" with the Nebraska Corn Board Association; Wyoming: Heulett - "National Park Service Ranger" at Devil's Tower National Park; Montana: Fishtail - "General Store Clerk" at Fishtail General Store; Idaho: Boise - "Real Estate Agent" with Re-Max Real Estate; Washington: Seattle - "Biologist" with People for Puget Sound Marine; Oregon: Medford - "Logger" with HM Inc.; Nevada: Las Vegas - "Wedding Coordinator" at Vegas Weddings; Arizona: Tucson - "Patrol Agent" with the US Border Patrol; New Mexico: Albuquerque - "Landscape Architect" with Hilltop Landscaping; Kansas: Topeka - "Meat-packer" with Fairview Farms; Missouri: Kansas City - "Boilermaker" with Boilermakers Local 83; Arkansas: Fayetteville - "Archeologist" with the Arkansas Archeological Survey; Oklahoma: Ringwood - "Roustabout" with A&T Roustabout; Texas: Houston - "Petroleum Engineer" with Chevron; Louisiana: New Orleans - "Bartender" at The Funky Pirate; Mississippi: Jackson - "Dietician" at Jackson Nutrition Clinic; Wisconsin: Theresa - "Cheesemaker" at Widmer's Cheese Sellers; Illinois: Chicago - "Transit Ticket Agent" at Metra; Michigan: Detroit - "Auto Mechanic" at Speedy Mechanics; Ohio: Cleveland - "Meteorologist" with Local NBC Affiliate; Indiana: Indianapolis - "Pit Crew Worker" with Panther Racing; Vermont: Cabot - "Sugarmaker" at Cabot Hills Maple; Kentucky: Versailles - "Horseman" at Three Chimneys Horse Farm; Tennessee: Nashville - "Studio Technician" at The Sound Kitchen; Alabama: Birmingham - "High School Football Coach" at Pelham High School; Georgia: Blakely - "Peanut Sheller" at Birdsong Peanuts; Florida: Orlando - "Park Entertainer" at Universal Orlando; South Carolina: Kiawah Island - "Golf Caddie" at Kiawah Island Resort; North Carolina: Greensboro - "Modeling Agent" with Directions, USA; West Virginia: Cambells Creek - "Coal Miner" at Selah, Inc.; Virginia: Charlottesville - "Gardens and Grounds" at Monticello; Maryland: Baltimore - "Cook" at Phillip's Seafood; Delaware: Wilmington - "Incorporating Specialist" at Corpora-

tions & Companies; Pennsylvania: Lancaster County - "Furniture Builder" at Paduch Country; New Jersey: Jersey City - "Child Counselor" at Boys and Girls Club; New York: New York - "Marketing Specialist" with Blueliner Marketing; Rhode Island: Newport - "Ambassador of Tourism" at Newport Visitor Center; Connecticut: Orange - "Insurance Broker" with Amity Insurance; Massachussetts: Brockton - "Baseball Scout" for the Brockton Rox; New Hampshire: Concord - "Political Party Worker" for the Democratic Party; Maine: Thomaston - "Lobsterman" at Branch Brook Farm; Alaska: Anchorage - "Photographer" with Clark Mishler Photography; Hawaii: Maui - "Surf Instructor" at Maui Wave Riders; California: Napa - "Cellar Master" at Domaine Carneros Winery.

Obviously, from even a cursory glance at the list, there's no way that Seddiqui was "qualified" for most of these, and jumped into many with virtually no training (for example, he took one day's worth of surf instruction before starting to *teach* surfing!). You really have to wonder what the folks who *hired* him were *thinking*, as his role at the vast majority of these wasn't even as involved as an *intern*, and he must have been, to most of the people working with him, more of a distraction than anything. In fact, he "walked away" from something like a half a dozen of these because he couldn't handle the working conditions, and you can imagine how happy his co-workers were to have him around!

I guess if there's one take-away here it's that "persistence pays" as, in nearly every case, the author was offering only the slimmest value to his employers (and in a couple of cases screwed things up badly), but he was able to badger, cajole, brow-beat, beg, and wheedle his way into 50 jobs in 50 weeks. Of course, one has to wonder, if these were going to be for *more* than a handful of maybe-paid days, whether he would have been as successful lining things up. I have a number of other quibbles with assorted things in the book, but they're more stylistic and editorial in nature, so I'll let them be rather than nit-pick.

50 Jobs in 50 States[4] just came out this month, so it should be available in your local brick-and-mortar book seller, but both Amazon and BN.com have it for around a third off, so that might be your best bet if this sounds like something you want to delve into. It certainly is *interesting* in scope, but I'm not sure (short of the "persistence" factor) there's much to learn here as the venture was so particular to the author.

Notes:

1. http://btripp-books.livejournal.com/109199.html

2. http://jobstalker.info/

3-4. http://amzn.to/21J3pQE

Saturday, April 2, 2011[1]

Words of wisdom ...

Here's another find I picked up at the Open Books[2] "box" sale a number of weeks back. As I noted at the time, I'm amazed that they don't have lines down the block for those sales, as they're *awesome*! Back in the '80s and '90's I was fortunate to attend a number of events featuring His Holiness the Dalai Lama, including the Kalachakra Initiation at Madison Square Garden in 1991. The talks in this book are from a follow-up visit to New York in the fall of 1999 during which the Dalai Lama gave a series of talks in various contexts around the city, culminating in a public event in Central Park, attended by a couple of hundred thousand people.

Because the Dalai Lama was addressing audiences of varying experience and exposure to the Vajrayana teachings, his choices of material ranged from the very basic to the rather advanced. This volume's editor, Nicholas Vreeland, did a *masterful* job of pulling together elements of these wider ranging teachings and preparing and unusually direct and focused document.

An Open Heart: Practicing Compassion in Everyday Life[3] is one of the most cogent looks at the Buddhist path (from a Tibetan Vajrayana perspective, of course) that I have encountered. As long-time readers know, I've read quite a lot of material in this tradition (sadly, I have *practiced* very little), and sometimes some books just don't grab me as the differences between what's in them and what's in my "knowledge bank" are sufficiently subtle that it comes out as "more of same". This book, however, follows a remarkable arc, clearly expounding ever-more complicated concepts and practices.

To give you a general sense of how the book progresses, here are the section titles: The Desire for Happiness; Meditation, a Beginning; The Material and Immaterial World; Karma; The Afflictions; The Vast and the Profound: Two Aspects of the Path; Compassion; Meditating on Compassion; Cultivating Equanimity; Bodhicitta; Calm Abiding; The Nine Stages of Calm Abiding Meditation; Wisdom; Buddhahood; and Generating Bodhicitta.

There can hardly be a better person to speak to Equanimity and Compassion than the Dalai Lama, as his life has been one of turmoil and horrific events. So, when he writes:

> This is how we come to see that our true enemy is actually within us. It is our selfishness, our attachment, and our anger that harm us. Our perceived enemy's ability to inflict harm on us is really quite limited. If someone challenges us and we can muster the inner discipline to resist retaliating, it is possible that no matter what the person has done, those actions do not disturb us.

This is not "platitudes", but the voice of experience of one who has had to suffer enemies, and maintained his spiritual calm!

As I don't operate in much of a Buddhist context, it's always useful to have "the basics" brought back to my attention ... one piece of this that stood out for me was on "developing ethical discipline":

> For Buddhists, ethical behavior means avoiding the ten nonvirtuous actions. There are three kinds of nonvirtuous actions: acts done by the body, actions expressed by speech, and nonvirtuous thoughts of the mind. We refrain from the three nonvirtuous actions of the body: killing, stealing, and sexual misconduct; the four nonvirtuous actions of speech: lying and divisive, offensive, and senseless speech; and the three nonvirtuous actions of the mind: covetousness, malice, and wrong views.

Needless to say, it would be a very constructive environment for practice where these "nonvirtuous" activities were avoided.

I felt rather churlish, when (in the section on Bodhicitta), I found myself wanting to raise objections to some of the examples that His Holiness was giving to illustrate how inter-connected we all are, and how we "depend" on others, however, I feel like I need to note this. At one point in this he says (as part of several examples) *"So much work has gone into providing us with the shirt we are wearing, from planting the cottonseed to weaving the fabric and sewing the garment."* ... and my reaction was that these steps all reflected *commercial self-interest*, and that were the farmer not envisioning making money on the cotton, he would not have planted and nurtured it, if the weaver wasn't planning on making a profit, he would not have bought the cotton and created fabric from it, and if the shirt-maker did not expect selling the product he would not have expended the effort ... so "providing" is probably something that triggered this response, as it brought up the example of [a pencil][4] by Milton Friedman. At no point in the creation of the shirt are the actions involved being done "selflessly", for my or any others' benefit, so, as an example to generate a feeling of connectedness, this runs up against what I'm assuming to be a "culture gap"!

Aside from my reaction to this one point, however, the rest of the book is excellent, and I would recommend it to anybody. I was quite surprised to see that [An Open Heart][5] is available via the new/used vendors for as little as a penny for "very good" copies of the hardcover (I have the paperback, which is still in print at a very reasonable cover price). This is one of those that I feel anybody would benefit from reading, so investing $4 (1¢ plus the $3.99 shipping for a used copy) is highly suggested!

Notes:
1. http://btripp-books.livejournal.com/109393.html
2. http://www.open-books.org/
3. http://amzn.to/1o90CD8
4. http://www.youtube.com/watch?v=d6vjrzUplWU
5. http://amzn.to/1o90CD8

Sunday, April 3, 2011[1]

Just say no?

A couple of weeks ago I attended a Social Media Club of Chicago event down at "the building formerly known as The Sears Tower" which featured Carol Roth as a speaker. I'd known *of* Carol for a while, having first encountered her via Jason Seiden's site, where they would do fun video features, and then started following her on Twitter (@Seiden[2] and @caroljsroth[3], if you're interested). Frankly, there had been so much discussion of her book, The Entrepreneur Equation: Evaluating the Realities, Risks, and Rewards of Having Your Own Business[4] (and her "action figure[5]"!) around there, that I'd assumed that it had come out *months* ago. However, at the SMC talk I learned that it was only "officially" coming out on 3/22, and I asked her about getting a review copy. Either her publisher or publicist is *very* on-the-ball, as I'd just *asked* on Wednesday evening, and the book appeared at my place that Saturday!

Now, I have to confess that I did not come to The Entrepreneur Equation[6] as a disinterested party. Both my parents had been entrepreneurs, I ran my own company for a decade, my wife had her own company, and I've worked for *other* entrepreneurs. In the current job market, the temptation to just "do it yourself" is very strong, as there are lots of extremely capable people "out on the street" who, for whatever reason, *can't* find a job. And, as regular readers of this space will realize, I'm presently in that category, now in my 23rd month of not having a regular job (although, thankfully, my freelance/consulting hours are growing).

This fact *strongly* colored my impression of Ms. Roth's book.

The web is swimming in complimentary buzz about this book, with quotes floating around along the lines of "The Best Book Ever on Entrepreneurship", and I had somewhat expected that this was going to be filled with material on what *"today's entrepreneur needs to succeed"*. While one can argue that the book *is* set up to prevent the would-be entrepreneur from *failing horribly*, it's in the manner that one can try to classify "*not* collecting stamps" as a hobby. I do not believe that there is *a single sentence* in this book *encouraging* entrepreneurial ventures. Not a one ... despite the fact that the government says[7] that *half* the private sector work force are employed by small businesses (and that's not even counting the "self employed"). Where do these businesses come from? Entrepreneurs. If you don't have entrepreneurs creating jobs, the *horrendous* job market would be that much worse. And, frankly, the "take-away" from The Entrepreneur Equation[8] it that pretty much everybody should never ever ever start their own business.

The "equation" of the title appears to be a series of self-assessments that Roth walks the reader through, assessments that I can't imagine one in a thousand people reading the book could honestly say "hey, that's for me!".

This book is a step-by-step tour of what can go terribly wrong in a business, and all the unpleasant things that running a business entails. At at each point, this is framed in relation to *leaving* one's current employment, with nearly *zero* attention given to the fact that there are vast numbers of people out there that *don't have that option!* I know several people who have, after years of beating their heads against the walls separating them from "real jobs", simply given up and started their own things ... because they could see no other alternative. I don't know what world Carol Roth is living in, but the plight of the highly-competent long-term unemployed doesn't seem to be on her radar ... maybe that's not on the curriculum when one's getting Magna Cum Laude at the Wharton School of Business.

Obviously, if you are wanting to "save" somebody from what you think will be a terrible mistake, this is the book to give them ... but there is not the slightest shred of "encouragement" here, with the one (somewhat bizarre in context) exception of an end-of-chapter recommendation of Timothy Ferriss' The Four-Hour Workweek[9] (which is as close to 180° from this for entrepreneurial vision as possible!). The focus of this book is why you *shouldn't* even consider starting a business, how the deck is hopelessly stacked against you (especially if you are currently employed in a nice job with dependable salary and benefits), and detailing, in gruesome particulars, what all can (and is likely to) go wrong. Again, if you *don't* have a job, I guess you're already written off. The closest thing that Roth might have as "hope" for the unemployed might be her lowest level of business types, the "jobbie", which involves taking something you're passionate about and trying to make some money at it.

This is one of the categories she puts businesses in, "The Jobbie", the "Job-Business", (Franchises - which she considers to be between these), and a "Bona-Fide Business". She sees "Jobbies" as useful as they allow (those currently employed) the opportunity to "test the water" with a product or concept to see if there might be a market for it, but she doesn't have much good to say for anything other than a major operation with lots of assets and layers of personnel.

I must admit, there were sections here which could have been written about my old publishing company ... both highlighting the problems I *knew* we had, and some others that I didn't. Oddly, this bothered me less than the somewhat blanket (a heavy, wet blanket) assertion that *"entrepreneurship is so different and challenging in today's environment than it was generations ago and ... the risks of starting, buying, franchising, and generally owning a business might not justify the potential rewards."*

I'm not saying that Ms. Roth's analysis isn't strongly reality-based, but that if *everybody* read this book, and took its assessments seriously, there would be maybe only ONE business starting for every *ten thousand* would-be entrepreneurs who considered it ... which would no doubt result in *massive* unemployment (by essentially removing the "small business" sector!) and some sort of dystopian governmental or corporate system coming in to pick up the slack ... or at least that's my take on this.

Anyway, if you (or somebody you think is unsuited to start a business) needs to be *talked out of their dreams*, by all means pick up a copy of The Entrepreneur Equation[10], as I can't imagine a more efficient tome for disabusing the vast majority of people from any hope of succeeding in business. This is, as noted, brand new ... so it should be out there in the remaining brick-and-mortar bookstores, but both Amazon and BN.com have it at 30-something percent off, so that would probably be your best bet if you were looking to check this out.

Notes:

1. http://btripp-books.livejournal.com/109591.html
2. https://twitter.com/Seiden
3. https://twitter.com/caroljsroth
4. http://amzn.to/1UOAzOw
5. http://theentrepreneurequation.com/doll/
6. http://amzn.to/1UOAzOw
7. http://www.sba.gov/content/small-business-economy-2010
8. http://amzn.to/1UOAzOw
9. http://btripp-books.livejournal.com/93466.html
10. http://amzn.to/1UOAzOw

Saturday, April 9, 2011[1]

Great stuff, but ...

This is another gem I picked up at Open Books'[2] wonderful "box sale" last month. This is an 1981 edition of Brad Steiger's 1971 Kahuna Magic[3], and wears its vintage prominently. In my various shamanic studies, I had encountered the *Kahuna* path (especially via Serge Kahili King's excellent *Urban Shaman*), and figured that I'd pick up this to see what Steiger had to say about it.

Steiger started writing for *Fate* magazine back in the 50's, and in the 60's and 70's he was extremely well known as a popularizer of various mystical and occult subjects, and as a "psychic researcher". A prolific writer, he has produced over 150 titles. This brings me to one point that I think I should note here ... there is *no way* that Steiger could have had in-depth *practices* in the wide range of subjects that he wrote about, so frequently his books are more "reporting" than systematic expositions of the inner workings of a tradition, practice, or group.

In the case of Kahuna Magic[4] Steiger's familiarity with the the Hawaiian "Huna" system comes almost exclusively from an old fellow, Max Freedom Long, who had contacted him in 1968 and convinced him to produce a "popular" volume synthesizing a lifetime's worth of research, which began with the material and concepts that he was introduced to by William Tufts Brigham, the retired director of a museum in Honolulu around 1920.

One of the points that Steiger makes several times through the book is that the native Kahunas "jealously guarded" their teachings, and only would pass them along father-to-son (even specifying that it had to be a "blood" son, not just some favored youth). Due to the colonization of the Hawaiian islands in the 1800s and the destruction of the native culture, by the time that some non-missionaries decided to take a look at this knowledge, it was hard to find.

If you notice a trend here, it's that one old white guy who'd studied a bit of the native culture passed on what he'd found to a young enthusiastic fellow, who (when *he'd* become an old white guy) then passed it along to Steiger. There is very little here which is explicitly sourced from a native practitioner, and *much* of it appears to come from "linguistic studies" where Long tried to wring out of the *words* used in the native language some sort of *belief system*. Frankly, much of what's laid out here has resonances with Theosophy, or even the teachings of Gurdjieff, which, given the lack of direct indigenous practitioners' input, is a bit of a warning flag as far as the authenticity is concerned!

That being said, the *system* presented here is fascinating. Most notable is the concept of the individual having *three souls* (operating within 3 "bodies"), which reminded me of the *Ba, Ka,* and *Akh* in the ancient Egyptian view. Unfortunately, the concept of "Lemuria" creeps in here as well, and

Steiger (or perhaps Long, it is sometimes hard to tell) postulates the Hawaiian culture pre-dating the other ancient cultures and providing a template for a wide array of belief systems. It is a shame that that sort of over-lay works its way into this, because the bits and pieces here have really remarkable parallels with various other traditions and lines of research. One of these is the idea that the "present" isn't a point but an averaging across a wider window, allowing influences to appear both forward and backwards without having a hard causality. Another would be a psychological model where "spirits" dislodge and get associated with the wrong body, bringing with them the specific baggage of their former place.

I guess there is a rather large literature looking into "Huna" (I actually ordered a couple of books to follow up on this), which would be all that more compelling if there were more input by traditional practitioners of the religion. At worst, this is a very attractive fusion of a wide array of western mystical threads with some specifics of the Hawaiian culture, with the possibility of being a rather remarkable approach to life.

Somewhat surprisingly, Kahuna Magic[5] is *still* in print forty years past its introduction, so it should be available (at least to order) from most book stores, and the on-line guys have it, of course. With the caveats raised above, I recommend this as an interesting look at a tradition that is still somewhat obscure.

Notes:

1. http://btripp-books.livejournal.com/109950.html
2. http://open-books.org/
3-5. http://amzn.to/1RyYPio

Sunday, April 10, 2011[1]

Carry the news ...

This was one of those "why haven't I read this before?" acquisitions, being "a classic" that one would have thought I'd have taken a look at previously. I'd seen it referenced somewhere and was putting in an Amazon order, and figured I'd "pull the trigger" on it. C.G. Jung's <u>Synchronicity: An Acausal Connecting Principle</u>[2] has been used over the years to bring "gravitas" to a lot of woo-woo, as Jung (who, after all, was following in the footsteps of other Great Men, such as Newton) was very interested in the mystical world, and in this volume made a specific study of things of that nature.

I don't know if "it's just me", however, but I found a good deal of this less than convincing, and that could be due to the fact that I've never "gotten" astrology, and an astrological survey is the backbone of the "hard research" done to support this book. Frankly, I don't even see astrology as a particularly "synchronistic" area of mystical pursuit, but the core data that he was working with were astrological tables produced for numerous married couples, and looking at various "conjunctions" and "oppositions" of the Sun, Moon, Mars, Venus, and "asc" and "desc" features which supposedly have favored data patterns for marriage. Again, none of this makes much sense to me (let alone when you get into footnotes like: *"Although the quartile, trine and sextile aspects and the relations to the Medium and Imum Coeli ought really to be considered, I have omitted them here so as not to make the exposition unduly complicated."*!!!). I take it that the data, as analyzed, ends up with improbably high "matches" for the individuals in the marriages ... or at least that's what I'm assuming the statistical number crunching is pointing at. I somehow can't imagine that others, with as little technical interest in or knowledge of the minutia of astrological charts as I have, would find this central section (about a quarter of the book) any more lucid than I did.

Much more interesting (and I really wish he'd concentrated more here) was how he related J.B. Rhine's work (with "ESP cards") to elements of his theory, as the data from those studies are much less arcane than the astrological material. Jung notes how Rhine's results were not effected by distance, and even (in certain experiments) by *time*, although they *were* effected by the mental state of the subject (early rounds where the reader was "fresh" tended to have much better results than later repetitions where fatigue/disinterest had set in).

Also fascinating is his on-going communications with the physicist Wolfgang Pauli (he of the "exclusion principle"). Jung and Pauli worked up a couple of theoretical frameworks in a "tetrad", where there were axes which went from space to time, with a perpendicular that went from causality to synchronicity ... which was then refined to one with "indestructible energy" on one end with "space-time continuum" on the other, and the causality/synchronicity axis across this (albeit with some added concepts).

Certainly Jung's interest in this area (and in the I-Ching and other systems), provided a legitimacy that occult practitioners have been trading on for decades. Here, however, is something of a summation of what Jung was specifically looking at:

> *Synchronistic phenomena prove the simultaneous occurrence of meaningful equivalences in heterogeneous, causally unrelated processes; in other words, they prove that a content perceived by an observer can, at the same time, be represented by an outside event, without any causal connection. From this it follows either that the psyche cannot be localized in space, or that space is relative to the psyche. The same applies to the temporal determination of the psyche and the psychic relativity of time. I do not need to emphasize that the verification of these findings must have far-reaching consequences.*

The copy I have of Synchronicity[3] is a recent edition, representing an effort to "spin off" bits of Jung's "The Red Book", by Princeton/Bollingen into new free-standing volumes (this being Volume 8 of Number XX in the Bollingen Series), so it has a 2011 Foreword, and is, no doubt available in the brick-and-mortar book vendors, with a cover price under $10 (not presently being discounted by the on-line guys). As disappointing as this is versus what it *could have been* (had the experimental focus been on something other than astrological charts), it's certainly an important book in the "mystical" field, and I'd suggest picking up a copy if this is of interest to you.

Notes:

1. http://btripp-books.livejournal.com/110231.html

2-3. http://amzn.to/1RmCXYr

Monday, April 25, 2011[1]

From the Ferenginar exo-cultural archives ...

This was one of those occasional books that arrives from a publisher with no contact, and no specific info (like a press release, etc.), which puts the "why" of it in question. The obvious answer is, of course, that I ended up on some list for my The Job Stalker[2] blog, and this was being sent out in the hopes of some coverage. Frankly, this is pushing the boundaries of what I find "useful" in my continuing education (let alone job search), and I was thinking of sorting it off to the wilderness of the "whenever" pile. However, I had recently seen it referenced in a couple of other "business" books that I'd been reading, so I figured "what the heck", as I'd not had a book to feature in that blog for a while.

How Companies Win: Profiting from Demand-Driven Business Models No Matter What Business You're In[3] by Rick Kash and David Calhoun is certainly not targeted to "the general reader", as it is very much a book for those involved in business and looking to update the way that their businesses do business. Beyond this, at several times in the reading, I got the sense that I was in the midst of a very large promotion piece for The Cambridge Group and/or The Nielsen Company as not insignificant portions of the book are case studies of work one or the other of the authors had done (it was not particularly clear which author was involved in which case) in rather self-congratulatory tones, with the main take-away being that they had some "magic formula" for re-focusing businesses.

Again, it's been a *long* time since I was "a suit" up in the Executive offices, so a lot of this was lovely theory, but nothing that I was presently in any place to put into action. I suppose that I should have run this past my hot-shot MBA brother, but my sense is that he doesn't read much, yet he is in the sort of operation that is target for the material in How Companies Win[4].

The main thesis here is that the concentration on the "supply chain" of previous generations has, both through the progress it has made to providing a vast plethora of product choices across many niches, and via the technological innovations of the web and mobile communications, and the societal changes that these have brought about, now become unreliable, and that companies need to look at the "demand chain" on almost a customer-by-customer basis. Key to this turn-about are the tools (perhaps *proprietary*?) to define "demand profit pools" via "demand landscape" analysis and thereby ferret out customer groups that have either not been specifically recognized, or are candidates for premium pricing strategies. Various "new definitions" are sprinkled through the book, here's one: *"Innovation is finding unsatisfied profitable demand and then fulfilling it."*

In another place they note that "the best and most competitive companies always feature some form of" what they call "mental modeling", which they define as: *"A mental model is the same picture in every employee's mind of how their company is going to compete and win – and their own role within that plan."*. Of course, as a "communications" guy, this looks pretty promising to me as it is no doubt going to involve constant and extensive programs of make sure that "every employee" is on the same page with management's "mental model"! Similarly, the following section caught my eye for obvious reasons:

> *Over the last few years, hundreds of millions of consumers around the world have used IMs, tweets, LinkedIn networks, fandom to popular blogs, and Facebook pages to organize themselves into brand-new social, political, and economic groups. These real and virtual communities and neighborhoods are remarkably sophisticated – and increasingly difficult for outsiders to enter. Do you understand the nature of <u>all</u> of the social groups to which your customers are now engaged? Do you have a strategy for reaching them in those locations – that is, gain entry? Do you have a way to assess your customers' need states while they are in those locations?*
>
> *Ultimately you and your competitors are in a race, and the winner will be the one who better satisfies the demand, in all of its forms, of your high-profit consumers. Many of the answers will be found in those new communities of your newly organized consumers ... <u>if</u> you know where to look and can gain entry.*

That, as much as what Gary Vaynerchuk wrote in The Thank You Economy[5], opens the door to a rather bright future for "digital natives", who will operate as Rangers making safe the way for the MBAs to get around to bleeding out the "high-profit consumers" that this book holds as the Holy Grail of the new business reality.

As How Companies Win[6] has only been out for a few months at this point, the odds are good that you might be able to track down a copy at one of few remaining brick-and-mortar book vendors with a business section, however, the on-line guys have it at around a third off of cover, and the "aftermarket" vendors already have *new* copies of the hardcover for only about six bucks. Again, this is pretty much a "specialty" book for folks in companies that manufacture and market products, but I guess anybody might find the case studies of interest, if just to have a peek into the internal workings of companies such as McDonalds, Hershey's, Budweiser, Best Boy, Allstate, Apple, and others that the authors have either worked with or studied!

Notes:
1. http://btripp-books.livejournal.com/110397.html
2. http://jobstalker.info/
3-4. http://amzn.to/1LIxsGG
5. http://btripp-books.livejournal.com/107420.html
6. http://amzn.to/1LIxsGG

Sunday, May 1, 2011[1]

Space songs on a spider web sitar ...

Last fall, my Wife and kids went down to visit my father-in-law in Arizona. It would have been fun to go along, but with my being in this seemingly-endless job search, it hardly seemed reasonable to pull me off the resume grind *and* have to figure out where an additional air fare would come from, so I stayed home. It sounded like they did some interesting things (unfortunately, having left the "designated family photographer" at home, they managed to have *deleted* all the pictures they took while down there when thinking they were "viewing" them), including going off to look at various petroglyph sites, where they picked up Kenneth J. Zoll's Sinagua Sunwatchers: An Archaeoastronomy Survey of the Sacred Mountain Basin[2] to bring back to me as a souvenir.

Over the years, I was fortunate to be able to travel fairly widely in the Southwest, having visited sites such as Canyon de Chelly, Chaco Canyon, Death Valley, Acoma Pueblo, Mesa Verde, The Grand Canyon, etc., and have binders of prints from various of these. When we've been down in Phoenix previously, I've dragged them off to the HoHoKam museum there, so they knew what would make Daddy happy.

However, I was a bit disappointed in Sinagua Sunwatchers[3], as it looked at first glance to be a rather in-depth consideration of a particular "solar panel" at the V-Bar-V Heritage site, but suffered from much of the "fuzziness" of the Archaeoastronomy field. The author congratulates himself for making a multi-month survey of the site (readings were made on the 21st of March, April, May, June, July, August, and the 22nd of September), which appears to be unusual, but it then brings up the question of how much *better* the information would be if the data was taken daily, and, perhaps, photographically captured at each point. Frankly, I'm somewhat ambivalent towards "Cultural Astronomy", as it always seems to invite reading in the observers' preconceptions into what is likely to be a rather limited data set (much in the way that a large sports stadium, given an even data distribution, is likely to average somewhere around 200 people with any particular birthday). At least in this case, the author limits himself to looking at the progression of a "sun shaft", or more realistically, two *shadows* being cast by projecting stones above the large (oddly, the physical dimensions don't seem to be given, even though the angular positioning, elevation, etc. are detailed), creating four "edges" which progress across the stone on the observed days, and through the year. This certainly provides "wiggle room" for interpretations, as you have edges *touching* glyphs (oh, and there are estimated to be over a *thousand* glyphs carved into this large flat standing stone), *crossing* glyphs, *bisecting* glyphs, as well as having elements of glyphs in the shaded areas, or in the lit areas. As you can guess, an eager devotee of this particular "science" could likely find *any* message on this stone if they worked hard enough on it.

The stone dates from anywhere from 600 to 1400 C.E., and was used by the Sinagua people who where predecessors of the Hopi, and (for various reasons) are postulated to have been the ancestors of the Hopi Water Clan. While Zoll attempts to weave in the mythos of the latter culture, it's pretty clear that the Kachina deity system (which he *irritatingly* insists on spelling *Katsina* here) didn't evolve until much later.

The author makes a case for particular glyphs and groups of glyphs having importance in relation to the agricultural cycle, with particular alignments indicating specific days, and I suppose that it's certainly *possible* that this is what the assorted carvings are indicating, but nothing here screams out "oh, look, this is the day when the sun stops and goes back" or other definitive astronomical notation. The fact that a pair of *lines* could easily have been etched in that which would have corresponded precisely to the edges of the "sun shaft" on the Equinox and Solstice and The Great Mythic Founder of the Tribe's birthday, or whatever, makes the "oh, look it's half the way down the snake next to the guy with the funny head" interpretation seem a bit weak.

To the book's credit, there is a reasonably cogent section on the science behind this, with angles of the Sun, Earth, orbital eccentricity, etc. explained, along with decent tables of data featuring the Solar altitude and azimuth on a minute-by-minute basis over the time of observation on the chosen days. It's just that there's nothing here like the "mid-winter sun shining down a shaft and illuminating a particular glyph/gem/burial on just that one day" sort of precision which would make all and sundry say "wow, how cool is that". No matter how much they fill in the tables here, they're still having to make claims that the back half of the glyph being in the light is significant versus the other glyph touching an edge of the other shadow … which leaves one wondering how much "science" there is in these observations.

Sinagua Sunwatchers[4] is available from Amazon new (and used from B&N), but is also available from the author's organization at http://www.sinagua-sunwatchers.com[5] … were you interested in helping to support their efforts. I found this "interesting enough" but (as you can gather from the above) not deeply convincing. If you're into things Southwestern, you'll probably enjoy this anyway, as it has enough history and cultural context to make it more than a one-trick pony.

Notes:

1. http://btripp-books.livejournal.com/110629.html

2-4. http://amzn.to/1pzwFgG

5. http://www.sinaguasunwatchers.com/

Monday, May 2, 2011[1]

slowly disappearing from my view

This book was a recent "win" for me in the LibraryThing.com "Early Reviewers" program, although how "early" it is, having been out for over half a year at this point (with a hardcover edition that carried a *cover price* of $116.95!) is something to be questioned ... perhaps the publisher is looking for readers to consider this much more reasonably priced paperback.

I'm not sure what I anticipated when requesting Hamid Dabashi's Iran, The Green Movement and the USA: The Fox and the Paradox[2], but it wasn't what the book ended up being. This is a strange package, with various sections each having a different tone, and most trying to fit into some part of a "teaching story" parable.

The book starts with a fable of the fox and the aging lion king, with Iran being the fox and the US being the aging lion. The central premise of the book appears to be that America has been lured into a place where no matter what it does in relation to Iran, it makes Iran stronger and damages our interests in the region. The author is *extreme* in his dislike of the Bush administration, which he argues to be evil, Christian Crusader, fascistic and stupid all at once (and if I wanted to hear that, I'd dial up CNBC). Obviously, a guy who came from Iran, got an advanced degree in Islamic Studies (OK, among other things) and ends up teaching at an ultra-liberal east coast university is likely to have a different view on the Middle East, but most of the front part of this book is a walk "through the looking glass" where the few points of sanity in the region are painted as demons and the bug-eyed lunatics are made to seem the good guys.

He does point out that the very regimes that previous US administrations had set up to be checks to the Islamic Republic of Iran have been the recent "regime change" targets in Iraq and Afghanistan, which has provided the Mullahs with a wide range of motion, both locally and through their influences across the region in general.

About halfway through the book, however, he changes gears and starts looking at philosophical questions, dragging up an opponent of Socrates, by the name of Thrasymachus, who appears to have argued that the true role of the citizen is to *oppose* the state, and starts building a case for the Green Movement having an organically integrated role in the Iranian *Republic*. This is put in context with a rambling look at Iranian political history, regional geopolitical trends, and various intellectual streams involved in both. He does a good job of disabusing the assumption that there is an inherent binary between the secular and the (fanatically) religious, basing this in large part in the romantic writings of various women involved in the movement. He posits a "cosmopolitan" culture which is the true underlying pattern for the Iranians, and that the current theocracy is as much an affront to that as anything, and traces how (utilizing assorted external "emergencies" the Islamists managed to eliminate all opposition and take over nominal control of the country. I say "nominal" here because it is argued that the present regime there lacks the legitimacy of popular support, and that the Green Movement is largely about returning to a multi-faceted "cosmopolitan" culture.

The further one gets into the book, however, the less Dabashi convincingly links it to parallels in the parables, and the more "professorial" his prose becomes ... here's a particularly egregious example:

> The internal dynamics of Islam itself has historically broken it down into its discursive, institutional, and symbolic forms (or, if preferred, its doctrinal, ritual, and communal formations) – all complementing or competing with each other, and contributing to make Islam a constitutionally multifaceted and cosmopolitan culture, and thus dialectically denying any one component to assume a dominant or exclusionary status. **Polyfocal** has always been the discursive disposition of Islam, just as the languages and cultures in which it speaks have been **polyvocal**, and the geographic domains and domesticities of its historical manifestations **polylocal**. The polyfocality of the Islamic epistemic cultures has spoken and written itself in conflicting **nomocentric** (the law-centered Sharia), **logocentric** (the reason-centered Falsafah), and **homocentric** (the human-centered Tasawwuf or Irfan) languages and lexicons.

One other interesting aspect (which he introduces, oddly enough, via a discussion on Cyberspace) is the multi-calendrical time sense in Iran, where "Persian", "Islamic", and "Western" calendars are overlaid on each other providing elements of symbolism which can be used in defiance of the imposed regime.

Again, the book sort of wanders, from an anti-US/Israel tirade at the beginning thought a look at the philosophical groundings of the Green Movement in the middle, to a rather "professorial" exposition of cultural elements at the end. The initial efforts to create parallels with classic teaching stories peters out, but is replaced by a parallel showing the oppressive Islamist regime in Iraq in pretty much the same position in relation to their own people as America is to Iran ... any action, hostile *or* accommodating, serves to weaken its stance and strengthen the opponent's. It never reaches much of any closure, but I guess that's to be expected, given the fluidity of the political reality in that part of the world.

This seems to be new in paperback, but it's not available at much of a discount anywhere (the after-market price no doubt driven up by the insanely-priced hardcover!), but I'm guessing you'd have to be pretty focused on the subject to want to "go there" anyway. I'm glad to have read this, as it certainly brought up stuff I'd not considered, but it's hardly a volume that I'd recommend to more than a handful of folks I know!

Notes:

1. http://btripp-books.livejournal.com/111090.html   2. http://amzn.to/1Ub39uE

Wednesday, May 4, 2011[1]

An interesting take on things ...

It's usually one of my rituals here to detail where a particular book came from or how it happened that I was reading it at that point. Obviously, with the current draconian FTC regulations on bloggers, this serves a purpose when a book was provided to me as a "review copy" and can be so noted, and I'm always happy to share the tales of "successful shopping" be that at the Dollar Store, a B&N on-line sale, one of the big Open Books[2] events, or even a particularly sweet deal through Amazon. I've wracked my brains over this one, however, and really don't have a clue how this got into my to-be-read piles ... it has been around for a while, and looks very likely to be "used", but I have no record of when it appeared. How odd!

Anyway, the *impetus* for me picking up a copy of Eckhart Tolle's A New Earth: Awakening to Your Life's Purpose[3] was to follow up on his The Power of Now[4], which I'd read several years ago. I recall not being "particularly impressed" with Tolle at that point, but he still had a lot of interesting points/perceptions, and I'm sure there was *something* out there which had pointed towards this book as something I should check out.

A New Earth[5] hardly made me a Tolle devotee, but it, like its predecessor, had enough quality bits that it kept me engaged through the reading, although my main take-away was that it was very uneven, swinging from fascinating conjecture to classic teachings to outright "woo woo" pretty much at whim. I must admit that, early on in this, he hooked me with *"The first part of this truth is the realization that the "normal" state of mind of most human beings contains a strong element of what we might call dysfunction or even madness."* ... although he lays this on "the Ego" (the book is largely a denunciation of the Ego) rather than so much on "the normals". Needless to say, I found this bit appealing:

> *All religions are equally false and equally true, depending on how you use them. You can use them in the service of the ego, or you can use them in the service of the Truth. If you believe only your religion is the Truth, you are using it in the service of the ego. Used in such a way, religion becomes ideology and creates an illusory sense of superiority as well as division and conflict between people.*

The most interesting part of this book is the concept of the "pain body", a "semi-autonomous energy-form that lives within most human beings, an entity made up of emotion", an accumulation of the remnants of old emotional pain and negative emotions that lives "within the very cells of your body". It is both individual and collective, with both single people locked into patterns of behavior and belief based on this residual pain, and nations and people acting out similar reactions, just writ larger. Perhaps counter-intuitively, the pain body seeks out pain, both in creating it in others and suffering it in the self, it feeds on "drama" and anguish and a whole spectrum of negative emotions ... it is what defines most of mass-media "entertainment", from bad people behaving badly to the concept of "if it bleeds, it leads". There are levels of density in pain bodies, from very faint traces in the nearly saintly, to dense masses in those people whose presence makes most people cringe.

Tolle suggests learning to recognize what "triggers" one's pain body so as to be able to avoid acting according to it's reactions. Obviously, having posited a fairly specific (if not unique) concept with this, he spends a good deal of the book weaving this idea into relationships with a wide range of teachings, putting a context around it to not have it seem as "made out of whole cloth" as it might standing on its own!

There are points here were he loses me, and I don't know if that's due a a failing on *my* end or that what he's spinning out requires more "connecting the dots" that I was willing or able to do. He begins talking about *consciousness* and how a higher level of consciousness is manifesting in the world, via those who are able to escape the snares of the ego and the pain body. He suggests that in most cases, only in age and death do we move through these levels and reach an awakening. Consciousness presses towards "awakened doing"...

> *Awakened doing is he alignment of your outer purpose – what you do – with your inner purpose – awakening and staying awake. Through awakened doing you become one with the outgoing purpose of the universe. Consciousness flows through you into this world. It flows into your thoughts and inspires them. It flows into what you do and guides and empowers it.*

There are three modalities of this, which he defines as acceptance, enjoyment, and enthusiasm, each being appropriate to certain situations. He also says that there are "frequency holders" developing whose task "is to bring spacious stillness into this world by being absolutely present in whatever they do", much like the classic "contemplative" role of various monastic disciplines. The "New Earth" of the title really is only briefly dealt with here, and it is the new conscious/spiritual reality being moved towards via the other elements discussed here.

Again, A New Earth[6] is *deeply* "newagey", and if you can't stomach that sort of thing, you're going to have a hard time reading this. However, what Tolle sketches here is very interesting and much of what he walks the reader through is *actionable* on a self-observing level. I'm not as thrilled with this as some (heck, this was featured by Oprah's book club!), but it certainly is a worthwhile read. The used guys have "very good" copies of the paperback for as little as a penny (plus, shipping, of course) and the on-line vendors have it at substantial discounts ... its popularity, however, probably means that it would be available via your local brick-and-mortar, if you're feeling like being kind to those folks.

Notes:

1. http://btripp-books.livejournal.com/111336.html
2. http://www.open-books.org/
3. http://amzn.to/1WKcXda
4. http://btripp-books.livejournal.com/34364.html
5-6. http://amzn.to/1WKcXda

Monday, May 16, 2011[1]

Changing your stories ...

Back in the '80s I did a good bit of archaeological and metaphysical traveling, and a significant chunk of this was on trips organized by Alberto Villoldo and (eventually) his The Four Winds Society. Interestingly (to me, at least), much of the material in his earlier books came from events on some of those journeys. Over the years his books (he now has a dozen or so out) have moved from being "journal-based" and into a more philosophical stance, and this is certainly in that mode.

While I am certainly *conversant* in the sorts of things that Alberto has been writing of late, I've probably not worked directly with him in the better part of a decade, so there is a degree of disconnect here, vs. when he was dealing with more specific "Incan" tribal shamanism of various stripes. Over the years his activities have spread out across a wider spectrum of native teachings and traditions and has come up with a non-specific "umbrella" name for these sources, "The Earthkeepers". While this, obviously, spares him a lot of "backgrounding" cultural details on his material here, and gives him a great deal of "wiggle room", I find myself wondering how much of what is owed to whom and how much of this is a newage amalgam arising from Alberto's workshops.

I had fairly high hopes for Courageous Dreaming: How Shamans Dream the World into Being[2], having recently read Steiger's Kahuna Magic[3], which had a substantial "dreaming reality" aspect to it, and I was hoping that this would involve similar concepts as expressed by a native tradition in which I'd had some training, perhaps something akin to those elements within the Castaneda corpus. However, this is more in the "new age workshop" vein, which is not necessarily a *bad* thing, but it wasn't what I was hoping for, and so did sort of "lose me" part way through.

Alberto frames Dreaming here, not so much in an otherworldly mode as in almost a "law of attraction" dynamic, with "dreams" being one's stories, and how these can be modified change the outcomes they are drawing in. He discusses some classic teaching stories and then defines "three stock characters" that he sees come up time and again in his consulting practice, that of "the bully", "the victim", and "the rescuer". These roles become important when you look at one's stories from a NLP (Neuro-Linguistic programming) stance, in that the repetition of one's stories reinforces the identification with those forms.

> *As you look at the seemingly unalterable facts of your life, you might say, "but I'm not making excuses. These facts are real." They may indeed be very real to you. However, it's easy to confuse the past with the present and the future, perceiving facts in a fixed reality when they may not be facts at all.*

> *Your "facts" are simply beliefs rooted in memories.*
>
> *Your brain doesn't distinguish between what's happening in the present moment and what you're experiencing as you retell a story about the past. Neuroscientists are discovering that at a synaptic level, a real and a recalled event both register in the neocortex and the limbic system in the same way, with the same intensity. ... In fact, every time you relive and old hurt, it reinforces that synaptic pathway.*

At this point he introduces the concept of the Luminous Energy Field (familiar to those who have read assorted shamanic books), and ties in this sort of reinforcement as cords within the LEF that will continue old, painful, destructive patterns long past their time. This then folds into the classic "four directions" elements, here envisioned as symbolic of four levels of consciousness, waking, dreaming, a lucid in-between state, and dreamless sleep, expressed as the *Eagle* - dreamless sleep or stillness, the *Hummingbird* - the dreaming state, the *Jaguar* - the lucid state between dreaming and sleeping, and the *Serpent* - our ordinary waking awareness. Each of these levels of consciousness has it's own form of "courage", the Eagle has *Spirit* courage, the Hummingbird has *Soul* courage, the Jaguar has *Intellectual, Moral, or Emotional* courage, and the Serpent has standard physical courage.

This takes us up to about 2/3rds of the way through Courageous Dreaming[4] and, frankly it's here that I started to get a bit lost (right at the point where "Part II: From Dreaming to Courageous Action" kicks in). This contains four chapters, "Courage as Action", "Practice Truth", "Clean Up Your River", and "Be Ready to Die at Any Moment" all of which have bits and pieces of classic new age and eastern wisdom, as well as the occasional shamanic practice, but I somehow found it very hard to follow. A good deal of this was based on what "the Earthkeepers believe" and less grounded in the approaches of the first half of the book. This could, of course "just be me" not connecting with a more symbolically structured modality, but it felt like having driven through a fascinating landscape smack into a thick fog bank to me.

Obviously, this might be more "for you" than it was for me ... again, it wasn't a "bad" book, but I'd gone into it hoping for something more specific and substantial, and ended up finding it a bit of a melange of many elements that were not necessarily finding a point where they were in sync. Courageous Dreaming[5] is only a couple of years old at this point, so could still be out in the brick and mortar vendors, but the on-line guys have it at about 1/3rd off of cover (and you can get a "very good" used copy of the hardback for under a buck). This is an *interesting* book, and could be quite appealing to those with pronounced "new age" sensibilities, so it might be something you'll want to check out.

Notes:
1. http://btripp-books.livejournal.com/111551.html
2. http://amzn.to/1S6qQOV
3. http://btripp-books.livejournal.com/109950.html
4-5. http://amzn.to/1S6qQOV

Tuesday, May 17, 2011[1]

Glad to read somebody else's adventures ...

This is another of the books I scored at the recent Open Books[2] "box sale" and is a bit of a departure from my regular reading. Tim Cahill is a travel/adventure writer, primarily for *Outside* magazine, as well as *Esquire* and *Rolling Stone*, and Jaguars Ripped My Flesh[3] is a collection of 30 of his articles covering a wide range of activities, conditions, and locations. The title is something of an *homage* to the 1950's "men's adventure" magazines, whose over-the-top use of gore and exclamation points were models that Cahill's publishers were hoping to avoid in the series of pieces they were asking of him, and he admits that there might have been a somewhat subconscious nod in there (via the *Rolling Stone* offices) to the Frank Zappa album of a similar name (this does not stand alone, by the way, as Cahill has additional collections that go by the equally traumatic titles of *Pecked to Death by Ducks* and *A Wolverine Is Eating My Leg*).

Cahill's writing has been compared to that of P.J. O'Rourke, and I think there are common threads of use of language and the ability to make what could be a somewhat monotonous first-person narrative sing with literary textures and masterfully expounded details. However, one must assume that on some level, Mr. Cahill is an adrenaline junkie. He discusses this particular creature (and the plumbing involved) in a section on climbing in Yosemite, but presents it in relation to the *other* climbers. However, from just *this* book, he has been in situations that would put off 99% of the population, especially as an on-going lifestyle. I would guess that a mere handful of the adventures and activities detailed in this book would be *quite enough* for most folks to spice up their life stories, and yet here he is with dozens (and only in one of several books).

As folks who have been reading my reviews over the years will no doubt realize, this sort of "adventure stories" is *not* one of my habitual genres, although I certainly appreciate the *idea*, and how it allows me to reflect on my more edgy journeys. However, I'm not sure how to best approach this in a review. It is, after all, a collection of discreet columns written for publication over a series of years in a handful of magazines; there's no unifying "quest", no political "theme", no search for any particular "truth", just situation after situation where the average guy might not have come out alive, presented in brilliantly descriptive prose.

Anyway, in Jaguars Ripped My Flesh[4] there are adventures with park wardens in Rwanda, dealing with Alaskan brown bears, the extended families of Peruvian mechanics, making a never-before-attempted rainy season climb on a 3,000-foot high South American waterfall, exploring uncharted ruins in Peru, attending a festival on an isolated Pacific island with a people fast losing their culture, a fascinating look into an equally fast-disappearing

Aboriginal ritual ground in Australia, hunting sea-snakes in the Philippines, lore of the porcupine in the West, filming gorillas in Rwanda, experiencing the butchery of sea turtles (and the political/economic factors around it) in Mexico, parachuting in California, hang-gliding off of a balloon in Montana, climbing sheer walls at Yosemite, taking a "Stormtrackers" flight into a hurricane, crawling through various caves, diving with sharks, Kayaking in Glacier Bay (amid Orcas), visiting ghost towns sucked dry by L.A., and the crowning story here: camping out across from Mt. St. Helens just weeks before it blew (his piece had managed to hit the newsstands just before the fact, and much of what he'd written was very prescient as to the actual events), and then returning immediately after. Again, any one or two of these would be enough "adventure" for most, but here Cahill is over and over in "might get killed" territory, and this is just one of *several* books!

If this sounds like a fun read (and I'm pretty sure it's more fun to read than to experience!), it appears to still be in print, with the on-line guys having it at about 1/3rd off its cover price, and the new/used vendors having "very good" copies for as little as a penny (plus, of course, the $3.99 shipping). These are fascinating, delightfully well written tales, although they may make your relationship with your couch more complicated, one way or the other.

Notes:

1. http://btripp-books.livejournal.com/111814.html

2. http://www.open-books.org/

3-4. http://amzn.to/1RkJa9v

Saturday, May 28, 2011[1]

Framing the Mayan culture ...

I was very excited to "win" this from the Library-Thing.com "Early Reviewer" program. "Archaeological travel" had been a passion of mine in my 20's and 30's, and I was fortunate to be able to visit a good number of sites around the world. The Mayan sites in the Yucatan were especially attractive, largely due to their proximity (a fairly easy flight to either Merida or Cancun), and I tried to get down that way at least once a year for a while there. Needless to say, I have quite a number of books on Mayan subjects in my library (a major factor in how the "almighty algorithm" of the LTER program decides who gets what book), and I would have been rather put out had I *not* been selected to review this.

However, Cities of the Maya in Seven Epochs, 1250 B.C. to A.D. 1903[2], by Steve Glassman and Armando Anaya, is a bit of an odd bird, as it were. The authors are both college professors, one from the U.S. And one from Campeche, but they set out to produce a book that *"would give an overview without getting lost in detail"* for a non-specialist reader. Glassman elaborates:

> *Almost all good books on the Maya are written by archaeologists (or Maya art historians). They know what they are talking about. The bad news is that archaeologists, almost without exception, write for other archaeologists. So, unless you are already versed in the topic, such as a graduate student of Mesoamerican (Middle American) archaeology or art history, it is virtually impossible to understand what the authors are saying. The book in your hands meets the needs of those with an interest in the Maya, but who have not yet developed a professional interest in the topic.*

I guess I should be flattered, as I'd never felt that it was "impossible to understand" what the authors of other books were saying, but I'd hardly say I have "developed a *professional* interest" in the Maya! Anyway, this goal on their part leaves the book out in something of a no-mans-land in terms of tone, more in-depth than what one might find in a popular magazine article or travel guide sidebar, but seemingly skittish when "in danger" of being too detailed.

The *concept* of the book is quite fascinating, however ... taking one city to represent a particular phase of Mayan (or pre-Mayan) culture and looking at that city from various perspectives, cultural, political, economic, and, of course, archaeological. One thing that really stood out, "conspicuous in its absence" were the typical wealth of graphics ... over 222 pages there were only sixty, of which 30% were maps, and while one graphic every four pages certainly qualifies as "illustrated", it's nowhere near what one usually sees in a book on Mayan ruins (plus, a significant chunk of the images presented were from INAH, the Mexican Government's "Anthropology and History" oversight organization, or even snapped from museum signs). I don't know if they were trying to avoid too much "art history" or "archaeology", but the dearth of author-originated images was hard to not notice.

Anyway, here's what's covered:

1. The Proto-Maya Olmec Cities of San Lorenzo and La Venta, 1250-400 B.C.: If Not the Mother Culture, and Undisputed Similar Culture.
2. The Mirador Basin in Times Long Gone, 1000 B.C. - A.D. 150
3. Tikal, the Eternal City, Early Classic, A.D. 250-550
4. Calakmul and the Snakehead Dynasty, a Maya Superpower
5. The Tale of Two Cities, Concluded, A.D. 695-869
6. Terminal Classic in the Yucatan, A.D. 800-1000
7. Mayapan, Tayasal, and Chan Santa Cruz

Obviously, in each of these "epochs" the information that's available is different. In the earlier chapters, there's pretty much just the archaeological record, when in later chapters, other sources are available. One of the more "less technical" aspects of the book is the biographical sketches spun out for various of the "discoverers" of ruin sites (I did not know that Charles Lindbergh had been a pioneer in aerial scanning for ruins, for instance), as well as background on a few Conquistadors whose fortunes were tied to those of assorted Maya cities. This was probably the "most valuable" information here (for me at least), as much of the discussions of the sites was more conjectural as to how they "might have been" when they were in their prime as opposed to heavy-duty analysis of the ruins.

Another fascinating bit is the events covered in the last part of the book. As you can see from the list above, there's no dating for the final chapter, but the sub-title indicates the span covered goes to A.D. 1903. This last section covers the time from the "post-Classical" Mayan world, through the invasion of the Spanish, and up into the revolution and temporary independence of the Yucatan in the mid-1800s. I had read a little about this latter phase, but nowhere near in as much detail as is presented here. Obviously, the authors believe that this was the most recent (final?) phase of Maya culture.

I would be interested to hear how somebody *not* particularly well-read on the subject of the Maya reacts to this book. To me, in trying to be non-technical, it also loses focus and is not for any particular audience (as one would think that somebody just discovering the Maya would want *lots* more pictures than are in play here). Cities of the Maya in Seven Epochs, 1250

B.C. to A.D. 1903[3] is also very steeply priced at $38.00 for an average length, no color plates, trade paperback. This is so expensive that I had to question whether this is being produced in typical press runs, or if it's coming out from a print-on-demand source. The on-line sources have this at full retail, and I'm wondering what sort of in-store distribution it's managed given the combination of factors noted here.

I enjoyed reading this, but I have hard time recommending it, especially at 3x what similar books might be going for. It's an "interesting" approach, with some very useful material, but unless you're a "Maya aficionado" (the very audience they were trying to *not* write for), I can't imagine this is something that you'd be happy with. "Your mileage may vary" (and it's certainly not a *bad* book), but it's sort of a book without an audience from where I sit.

Notes:

1. http://btripp-books.livejournal.com/112084.html

2-3. http://amzn.to/1XN9DOo

Sunday, May 29, 2011[1]

An AWESOME book for the job search!

Wow. As regular readers of this space know, I've been involved in various job searches over much of the past decade, and I'm *amazed* that this book (despite having gone through many on the same subject) never came to my attention before now, in its 6th edition. Frankly, had the good folks over at Ten Speed Press not sent me a review copy out of the blue, I'd likely have not found this on my radar now. However, Mark Emery Bolles (with his father, Richard Nelson Bolles, of the "Parachute" publishing empire) has written a truly amazing book, What Color Is Your Parachute? Guide to Job-Hunting Online, Sixth Edition: Blogging, Career Sites, Gateways, Getting Interviews, Job Boards, Job Search Engines, Personal Websites, Posting Resumes, Research Sites, Social Networking[2] (yeah, I know, that's one big honking title!).

As regulars also know, over the past year and a half I've been writing *The Job Stalker*[3] blog over at the Chicago Tribune's "ChicagoNow" blogging site, a vehicle that's focused on the view of the job search from somebody enmired in same (and I've just passed my *24th month* in my current job search). My focus, since taking over the blog in late 2009, has been on using on-line resources, and this book would have been a godsend on those weeks when I didn't have much of anything to write about! I suspect that my "wrangler" over at ChicagoNow would have *loved* to have had this guy writing that blog instead of me … as this is chock-full of all that good information that had managed to escape my notice.

One thing that I'm excited about is that this is "brand new", having just officially debuted less than two weeks back, so the info in here didn't have any of those "temporal cringes" that so quickly creep into books about the web … yet, at least. I am, however, somewhat chagrined at how much of the stuff in here *I had never heard of*. There I am, dispensing opinion on things job-search related, and all this stuff is out there that I totally didn't know. I mean, I sort of do *now*, but geez. While much of Job-Hunting Online[4] is "list oriented", it's not all endless entries of places to go (although, Bolles does provide this very handily in the companion web page: http://job-hunting-online.webs.com/[5] which *already* has a couple of dozen updates as of a 5/1/11 posting), but there's a lot of job search "philosophy", interesting data, and wry humor involved.

One of the more shocking (if one stops to think about it) figures he presents in an early chapter here is that the average *job* only lasts three and a half years, while the average *job search* takes 33 weeks (with those looking for more senior positions looking at a one-to-two year search). This would mean that the "average worker" has to figure on having a job search for more than a half year out of every four year period of their working lives … and how many folks are putting 1/7th of their income away for *that* likelihood?

Bolles has a particular dislike for the "big boards", assuming a level of dependence on these that I, personally, have not been tempted to nor seen in various networking with other job seekers. However, he constantly revisits the figures for getting employed via these ... which range as low as .4 and as high as 4% (although some claim 10% results). One of the more interesting things here is his reporting on the success rates for various approaches. Given that "using the major sites" had such a low success percentage, the following (in the introduction to a thing about "Job Clubs", which I'd never previously heard of):

> *Here's an interesting little tidbit: one of the most successful ways of find a job is by picking up the phone book, calling around to the businesses listed in the fields you are interested in, and asking if they have any job openings. This method of job-hunting is listed as having an 69% success rate (meaning that out of a hundred people who use only this method in their job-hunt, 69 of them will be successful). Now, this is the interesting part: if you do exactly the same thing, but you do it as part of a group of people who are all job-hunting this way, the rate of success jumps to 84%.*

Amazing, eh? Not only do the numbers suggest that "cold calling" has success rates 17-21 *times* that of the big boards, but that Bolles assumes that some people still have and use *yellow pages* (and he does highly recommend the actual hold-it-in-your-lap dead tree yellow pages)!

Job-Hunting Online[6] is arranged in several chapters, each with a wide array of sub-sections, the main ones are: Skills, Resumes, People, Research, and Job Boards, with additional material in the introduction and chapters labeled "First" and "Last". Again, there is *so much in here* that I could be blithering on for *pages*, but suffice it to say, I was *blown away* by this resource.

Obviously, if you are looking for work, or know somebody who is, I'd enthusiastically encourage you to go out and *buy this book*. As far as I can recall at this point (having just finished reading it), this is the *best* book I've encountered for charting one's path through the job-search, especially utilizing the internet. The depth and breadth of content in Job-Hunting Online[7] is truly amazing, and the on-line book mongers have it discounted to under ten bucks. This is definitely one that everybody looking for work needs to have sitting on their desk!

Notes:

1. http://btripp-books.livejournal.com/112226.html
2. http://amzn.to/1S6ocbM
3. http://jobstalker.info/
4. http://amzn.to/1S6ocbM
5. http://job-huntingonline.webs.com/
6-7. http://amzn.to/1S6ocbM

Tuesday, May 31, 2011[1]

A refreshing read ...

Here is one of those rare books that I actually bought *at retail* (well, at a 40% discount off of cover, but hey, it wasn't used, from the dollar store or a clearance sale, or a review copy!), which is, I suppose a bit of a testimony to the author in and of itself. Sam Harris is, of course, one of the leading voices of disbelief, one of the main faces of what one dares hope to be a "new Enlightenment" against the myth-based darkness of moronic religiosity on one hand and socialist totalitarianism on the other. His book The Moral Landscape: How Science Can Determine Human Values[2] takes both a look at how "morality" can stand outside the crippling morass of religion, and how science could well be on the cusp of having measurable means of determining what is or isn't moral.

As much as I am enamored of this book and its author, I feel a need to throw some "editorial finger-wagging" in at this point. I was feeling, about 2/3rds of the way through reading this, that it really wasn't "hanging together" as a book, and was wondering why the assorted sections varied so much in tone and structure. It was only *after* getting through the book (and its extensive footnotes) that I hit the "Acknowledgements" pages and found that this was, in large part, based on a handful of academic papers that Harris had published in his "day job" in Neuroscience, and especially in regards to research he's worked on in "neuroimaging" brain states. This was an "Aha!" moment, as some of the parts of this run towards the very technical, and are rife with footnotes pointing to research papers that, frankly, no one is likely to have much interest (unless they too were neuroscientists) in following up. An "About This Book" page up front (before the chapter-length Introduction) that set out that parts of this were from various research studies, and parts of it were "weaving this all together", would have made the subsequent "unevenness" of the book both understandable and expected (rather than my initial response that "gee, he doesn't do so well at writing long-form, does he?").

The book is broken up into six sections, an over-view introduction on "The Moral Landscape" which takes a look at various historical contexts of morality, then chapters on "Moral Truth", "Good and Evil", "Belief", "Religion", and "The Future of Happiness". These vary on how dependent they are on the scientific background, and how much "philosophy" (there's a 2.5 page footnote just dealing with Catholic pedophilia in "Moral Truth" section that is a fascinating read on its own) there is at core.

Generally speaking, Harris makes a case of there being a base-line for morality, linked to the concept of "well-being" of conscious creatures. While this has variable levels (what of whales, dolphins, chimps, dogs, cats, pigs?) which can be argued, the question of what provides the most well-being to humanity seems to be the central concern. Here is as close, I think, as he comes to an over-all statement (from the "Good and Evil" chapter):

> *I believe that we will increasingly understand good and evil, right and wrong, in scientific terms, because moral concerns translate into facts about how our thoughts and behaviors affect the well-being of conscious creatures like ourselves. If there are facts to be known about the well-being of such creatures - and there are - then there must be right and wrong answers to moral questions. Students of philosophy will notice that this commits me to some form of moral realism (vis. moral claims can really be true or false) and some form of consequentialism (vis. the rightness of an act depends on how it impacts the well-being of conscious creatures). While moral realism and consequentialism have both come under pressure in philosophical circles, they have the virtue of corresponding to many of our intuitions about how the world works.*
>
> *Here is my (consequentialist) starting point: all questions of value (right and wrong, good and evil, etc.) depend upon the possibility of experiencing such value. Without potential consequences at the level of experience - happiness, suffering, joy, despair, etc. - all talk of value is empty. Therefore, to say that an act is morally necessary, or evil, or blameless, is to make (tacit) claims about its consequences and in the lives of conscious creatures (whether actual or potential). I am unaware of any interesting exception to this rule. Needless to say, if one is worried about pleasing God or His angels, this assumes that such invisible entities are conscious (in some sense) and cognizant of human behavior. It also generally assumes that it is possible to suffer their wrath or enjoy their approval, either in this world or the world to come. Even with religion, therefore, consequences and conscious states remain the foundation of all values.*

To a large extent, the book expounds on this basic concept, of what does or does not promote well-being. Of course, this being Sam Harris, he gleefully takes numerous broadsides at the ludicrous aspects of religions and those who believe in them, and these are, naturally, some of my favorite parts (it is only with great restraint that I'm not quoting large blocks of rather florid text aimed at the Catholic church, or the far more pointed bits given over to the viler aspects of Islam).

As one might expect from Harris' scientific background, there are *fascinating* parts here of the functioning of the human brain in relation to assorted "moral" input, from classic behavior experiments to his own work with scanning equipment to see what is active at what point given what conditions. Aside from his own research, he encapsulates a great deal of other material here, from that which questions "conscious" acts (where the body begins an action well before the mind "decides" to take that action), to differences in behaviors in various cultural categories. He also takes a few shots at other scientists who seem to attempt to bend over backwards to "play nice" with religion, or to justify faith-based stances, and tears up their arguments with aplomb.

I rather enjoyed The Moral Landscape[3] and would recommend it to anybody with an interest in "how we work", as it is quite a look "under the hood" as it were, both from the philosophical perspective and the hard data of brain scan sciences. This has only been out about a half a year, so the "used" guys don't have deals at this point, but the hardcover is currently available for 40% off, and the paperback can be had for under ten bucks. It's certainly not for everybody, but it's a fun and interesting read.

Notes:

1. http://btripp-books.livejournal.com/112564.html

2-3. http://amzn.to/1pyHW0F

Monday, June 6, 2011[1]

No, pie are ROUND!

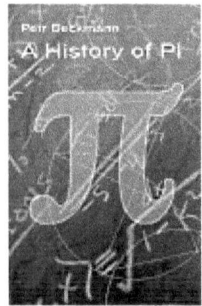

Please pardon the pun, it was the only way to get it out of my head (say it like Cookie Monster for best effect).

This is another of the books that I scored at the most recent OpenBooks[2] "box sale" (I really did *very* well with that, despite splitting the box with my daughters and one of their BFFs!). Petr Beckmann's A History of PI[3] is well known, having been kicking around since 1971, but possibly more for its reputation of being somewhat cantankerous than for its research.

Beckmann has an interesting biography, having fled his native Czechoslovakia ahead of the Nazi invasion, his family spending the war years in the U.K., where he flew with the R.A.F. In a Czech squadron. After the war he returned to Czechoslovakia (now on the other side of "the iron curtain") and completed a doctorate in Electrical Engineering. In 1963 he managed to get invited to join the faculty of University of Colorado and moved to the U.S., became acquainted with Ayn Rand, and functioned as a contributing editor of an Objectivist publication. I usually wouldn't background an author like this, but there are aspects of his writing which make considerably more sense in context. Two things constantly draw his ire, "militaristic" states (be they Rome, the Nazis, or the Soviets), and Religion. You might well ask, *"What do those have to do with π?"* to which the answer is "not all that much, really" (well, except for Fundies who want to make π equal something other than what it does, based on some vague biblical twaddle in 1 Kings VII.23). However, this does not stop Dr. Beckmann from constantly firing off broadsides at his favorite targets while tracking the historical development of π.

This is one of those books which would have been *vastly* improved by involving a real editor ... while not so much as in the cliché cases of Doctors and Lawyers who act that role for themselves, this is a case where "being his own editor" made the resulting book a far, far weaker venture than might have been the case with some less reactive voice saying "no" where necessary!

While reading this, it occurred to me that Dr. Beckmann was "a man before his time", as the chapters in this book would have been *much* more effective as posts to a website ... frankly, on some levels, it substantially reminded of parts of Richard C. Hoagland's site[4] ... and Beckmann could have ranted continuously on the web, were he not under the constraints of putting ink on paper. The book certainly *reads* like a "fringe" site, where the author clearly knows quite a bit about his subject, but is taking that knowledge into justifiably uncharted territory.

The "meat" of the book, however, is pretty solid. He starts with a look at human culture, and posits a "belt" where agriculture developed and allowed people to have specialized roles, including those involving numbers. He looks at how π was likely approximated by various cultures, the Babylonians, the Egyptians, the Mayans, ancient Chinese, etc. with only the occasional predictable (and fully justified) slams at religion where it intentionally eradicated the amassed knowledge of entire cultures (as with the Maya, Aztecs, and Incas).

He then moves to the Greeks, and discusses several leading lights, some well known, some less so. Here too he is not shy in expressing his dislike of some (Aristotle) and his extreme admiration of other (Archimedes). However, when the discussion rolls around to Rome, he lets fly:

> Rome was not the first state of organized gangsterdom, nor was it the last, but it was the only one that managed to bamboozle posterity into an almost universal admiration. ... They have been led to believe that the Romans had attained an advanced level in the sciences, the arts, law, architecture, engineering, and everything else.
>
> It is my opinion that the alleged Roman achievements are largely a myth; and I feel it is time for this myth to be debunked a little. What the Romans excelled in was bullying, bludgeoning, butchering, and blood baths.

He constantly refers to the Romans (and the likes of Caesar) as "thugs" and frequently draws parallels to the Soviets.

Needless to say, moving forward into The Dark Ages, he doesn't become any kinder to the Church of Rome, which made a habit of torturing and murdering practitioners of Science as though they were toiling in "Dark Arts".

If there is one thing this book is good for, it's a survey of prominent mathematicians over the years. Much of the structure of the book is looking at how various of these had addressed π and moved forward with the precision of its determination as well as methods for its calculation. I was, frankly, surprised at how many different ways one could come up with π, and how many people had made strenuous efforts to push forward the number of known places (a graphic at the end of the book reproduces a computer print-out of the first 10,000 decimal places of π).

The author also spins out assorted mathematical trivia that one might not know (I didn't) like the Greek letter "π" was not used until fairly late in history, and was derived from "periphery", and that "sine" in the measurements of angles, etc., came from a mis-translation where a Hindu term had been translated into Arabic, and the Latin translation from that assumed a wrong vowel amid the written consonants, and came up with "bay", which then got made into "sinus" ... having no relation to the original term which meant something along the line of "half-chord".

The book is also quite full with chunks of fairly advanced math. I'm a bit of an "untutored" math fan, and was lost from the get-go here. However, Beckmann suggests that the non-specialist simply ignore those parts, and I (like most, I assume) did so.

Amazingly, A History of PI[5] is still in print 40 years on, with a paperback edition that the on-line guys have at over a third off, and under ten bucks, however the used vendors have "like new" copies of the hardcover edition that I have for as little as one cent (plus shipping, of course), so this could be had for cheap. I'm torn on this ... I'm glad to have read this as a historical overview, but irritated at it at the same time (and the math just flew by over my head) ... if it sounds like "your thing", by all means pick up a copy, but this sure isn't an "all and sundry" recommendation!

Notes:

1. http://btripp-books.livejournal.com/112684.html
2. http://www.open-books.org/
3. http://amzn.to/20SEHST
4. http://enterprisemission.com/
5. http://amzn.to/20SEHST

Tuesday, June 7, 2011

A French Curry?

I really wanted to like Huna: Ancient Hawaiian Secrets for Modern Living by Serge Kahili King more than I did, as his book *Urban Shaman* is one of my favorites on practical Shamanism. However, after following up reading Brad Steiger's Kahuna Magic with some additional on-line research, I have some lingering doubts about the whole "Huna" tradition. One of the things that keeps coming up is the deep insularity of the native Hawaiian culture, and how their mystical practices were kept very close to home, typically only transmitted father-to-son, and that the majority of "what we know" about these practices come from one "white guy" who passed it along to another "white guy", who then tried to tease out "secrets" from the language itself, and create a "system" of the material at hand.

Into this channel comes Serge King, another non-Hawaiian "white guy" who, like the others in this tale, becomes fascinated with the "Huna" teachings and starts to investigate it. To his credit, King does not sit in an office and try to figure out what the words might have "really meant", but found teachers within the culture, the Kahili family who "adopted" him and "trained" him for over 20 years. As is always the case in these situations, it is VERY hard to determine what is straight-out "history" and what is convenient myth-making (and, as more dedicated readers will realize, is a *significant* issue in my own "Shamanic lineage"). There are many natives who totally reject what the various writers on this subject have presented as "Hawaiian", casting various aspersions on it as being "Theosophy in a hula skirt", etc. (I really don't want the mental image of Madame Blavatsky dancing in a grass skirt with a coconut shell bra!). However, as somebody trained in a far more "open" Shamanic tradition, I see stuff in what King is presenting which is very solid. So, I'm somewhat "on the fence" on the subject of the legitimacy of what's here.

In any case, the material in this book would make a *superb* "new age" weekend seminar (and I'm sure it regularly is sold this way), as it's clear, coherent, and practicable. In a genre which is full of embarrassing woo-woo, these are very good things to be. To give you an idea of what's operating here, this is the list of the "seven principles of Huna":

1. The World Is What You Think It Is
2. There Are No Limits
3. Energy Goes Where Attention Goes
4. Now Is The Moment of Power
5. To Love Is To Be Happy With
6. All Power Comes from Within
7. Effectiveness Is the Measure of Truth

Again (and I think "obviously"), these do *not* sound like the concepts of any "native culture" that I've experienced or studied. These sound very much like the philosophies of the early forebearers of the current "laws of attraction" movement, and, frankly, King does not spend too much space trying to insist that these are unsullied ancient native wisdom teachings ... he sets this up within the context of his white predecessors' work, and frames it within his teachings with the Kahili family, but only spends the first 1/6th or so of the book doing so. The rest of the book is pretty much "OK, here's this system, and here's how you make it work for you today".

As I noted, I have been very impressed in the past with Serge Kahili King's writing on Shamanic *technique*, to the extent that his *Urban Shaman* is one of the main books I recommend on the subject. Given this, I am quite sure that he *did* study with native teachers, and that he absorbed quite a lot of very specific knowledge in the process. I am also reasonably sure that whatever "newagisms" that are in this have been carefully focused to at least hew closely to the lines of the philosophies that he absorbed from these teachers. However, I seriously doubt that what is presented in Huna: Ancient Hawaiian Secrets for Modern Living[4] is a "native practice" the way that something like the Afro-diasporic faiths such as Ifa are in relation to their source cultures. Does this invalidate the content here? Not as a practice "for Modern Living" (as per the sub-title), but where I am willing to claim having been trained in "Incan" Shamanism (as my teachers were clearly of this lineage, if tribally Quechuan or Q'ero), I would be hesitant to label what is presented here as "Ancient Hawaiian Secrets". I am reminded of what famed Chinese chef Ken Hom once described as "French curry" (a liter of heavy cream with one teaspoon of curry powder) as it relates to actual Indian cuisine ... Huna[5] may be doing homage to its sources, but it really is a whole different thing.

However, as noted, as a "newage" training manual, Huna[6] holds together as a reasonable, cohesive system, and does not embarrass itself by veering off into the "silly zones". It may be a "French curry", but it's still a very attractive dish, if one is willing to let it be "native inspired" rather than an authentic Hawaiian cultural artifact.

Huna[7] is a few years old, but is still in print, and the on-line guys have it at a reasonable discount (oddly, the new/used vendors don't have it at much cheaper, once you figure in the shipping). If you're *looking* for "something like this", you could certainly do worse than this book, but if you're looking to study "Ancient Hawaiian Secrets", I'm afraid you're likely to be (as I was) somewhat disappointed.

Notes:

1. http://btripp-books.livejournal.com/113030.html

2. http://amzn.to/20SDMSk

3. http://btripp-books.livejournal.com/109950.html

4-7. http://amzn.to/20SDMSk

Friday, June 17, 2011[1]

My kind of town ...

Oh, my ... a book purchased at *full retail* at an actual *store* (with sales tax and everything) ... what *is* this world coming to?! I picked up a copy of Carl Smith's The Plan of Chicago: Daniel Burnham and the Remaking of the American City[2] over at the Chicago History Museum after a largely fruitless visit to get Daughter #2 up to speed on her Social Studies Fair project on "the Burnham Plan". While they had *a copy* of the original Plan book on display, that was pretty much all they had on this, so I was forced into "plan B" (for the "B. Plan" ... heh!), and, not wanting to invest $85 in the centennial facsimile edition, picked up this to tide her over. Now, at age 11, she really wasn't particularly interested in *reading* it, but she looked at the pictures, scanned over parts, and felt that she'd gotten what she needed (a non-web source?) out of it.

I'd always known *of* "the Burnham plan", but really didn't know much about it, except for that it was the source of the idea that Chicago should have parks up and down its lakefront, as opposed to the shipping you see in Milwaukee, or the heavy industry you see in Gary. Being a "city boy" my whole life, and living first in Lincoln Park and then the Gold Coast, the lakefront park system (and museums, etc.) have been a great boon, and I was quite appreciative of the fact that these were *planned* features. I did not know, however, how *extensive* the plan had been, and, realistically, how *little* of it had actually been implemented.

Officially simply titled *The Plan of Chicago*, it was published on July 4, 1909. It was spurred on by The Commercial Club of Chicago, which included most of the leading businessmen of the day (and familiar names of present-day streets and cultural institutions). Most of the center of the city had been destroyed in the Great Fire of 1871, and what had been built to replace what had burned was frequently "fast and cheap" construction, into which a rapidly escalating population crammed itself. Conditions for the average worker were horrible, and even with the reversal of the Chicago River (so that sewage and industrial effluent would not end up in the Lake where the drinking water came from) in 1900, there was still highly unsanitary housing for many if not most of the population. The "City Fathers" took a paternalistic interest in this situation, and determined that something seriously needed to be done before the city lost its appeal as an evolving metropolis.

Architect Daniel Burnham had been a key figure in the development of the World's Columbian Exposition of 1893, creating the fantastic "White City" of that fair. This, and other planning work that Burnham had done, inspired the Commercial Club to develop a plan for Chicago, and worked with Burnham, and his associates, to create "The Plan of Chicago". It is somewhat telling how little the *official* government of the city and state were involved with this

... as the corruption of the day was, if possible, even worse than it currently is. The Commercial Club and Burnham brought the message and vision directly to the people, and (while keeping the politicians at least nominally "in the loop") created a demand for the project that could not be ignored.

The full plan was, while being focused on making life better for the "common man", rather elitist in its particulars. Largely inspired by the planned developments of Paris and Washington, DC, it has a look-and-feel that, to the modern eye, evokes images of Speer's *Germania* more than anything. It is somewhat ironic that it was likely the First World War that derailed the plan from being implemented as Burnham and his allies envisioned. Most notable is what was intended to be the center of the new city, a *HUGE* domed structure to be City Hall at the focus of wide radiating avenues. This would have been at Halsted and Congress (with Congress being the main east-west line of the city), *right* where the current "circle interchange" is!

One element that did get implemented is the bridge that connected Michigan Avenue south of the river with Pine Street north of the river, with the double-decker structure that allowed for deliveries, etc. to keep to the lower levels. Without this Chicago wouldn't have the iconic Michigan Avenue. The general plan for Grant Park was put in place as well, with some of the museums .... although today's Navy Pier was only *one* of two planned for the lakefront. Interestingly, the Plan lives on in the Chicago Plan Commission, and related organizations, which take an active role in what gets built, torn down, developed, etc. in the city.

Smith's The Plan of Chicago[3] is an interesting history of a particularly key point in Chicago's development and a fascinating look at the men who were dedicated to charting its future. It had lots of maps, illustrations, vintage photos, and plates from the Plan (in b&w), which give you a view of parts of the city long gone. The book is available from the on-line guys at a reasonable discount, putting it under $10 to pick up. If you have an interest in city planning, turn-of-the century business, architecture, or just a fascination with Chicago, you'll be happy to have this on your bookshelf.

Notes:

1. http://btripp-books.livejournal.com/113393.html
2-3. http://amzn.to/1mze8PC

Sunday, June 19, 2011[1]

Dead people's books ...

Today's volume found its way into my hands via the famed Newberry Library Book Fair, which we attend pretty much every year (typically on "half-price Sunday"). One of the things I've noticed about the Newberry sale versus the ones at After-Words or Open Books is the significantly higher percentage of material on hand is very clearly "estate" left-overs. It seems that, unless one has a "willable" library (my Mom, several years before her death, gave her extensive collection of cookbooks and other "foodie" books to the Home Ec program at her alma mater), upon one's demise it will either be descended on by assorted "vultures" (my Father's library was quickly picked clean by grad students) or be "disposed of" by various means. I frequently get into message-board jousts with assorted folks over on LibraryThing.com about the utility of having a "price" range in the data, as "replacement value" for a library is something that can be negotiated with insurance companies (itemized for any particularly valuable volumes), but has very little relation to "resale value". I found, when dealing with my Mom's estate, that the folks who were quoting options for auctions, etc. pretty much ignored the books, or (at best) were willing to value them at something like a dime each, hardly what the book-lover imagines when gazing upon his or her assembled collection. Anyway, what happens frequently in downtown Chicago is that the shelves will be emptied into boxes and dropped off at Newberry (although I think Open Books is seeing a lot of this supply these days as well).

The reason for this long prologue here is that the current volume is not only reasonably *old* (from 1964), but has an "ex libris" bookplate up front. Now, for many years, I *hated* to get used books because I didn't want to have "dead people's stuff", but (after a decade of extremely "reduced circumstances") I eventually got used to the "used" channel being my primary book source, and I find it fascinating when I find "historical" stuff in the book. As I've noted here in these cases, I like to do some research on the names, just to know *which* dead person had this before me. In this case, the original owner was one Emil M. Lesza, who appears to have died in 1991 (B: 1913), however, my guess is that a Lawrence Lesza (his son?) had kept the book when Emil died, as *he* expired in 2010 (B: 1950) ... which would be just the right time-frame for the book to have found its way to the Newberry Library for last year's book fair.

Anyway, the book in question is Wolfgang Cordan's (a pseudonym, I discovered) Secret of the Forest: On the Track of the Maya and Their Temples[2]. Once more, a bit of background might help put this in context, Cordan (Heinrich Wolfgang Horn) was a German who fled the Nazis and fought with the resistance in Holland. After the war, he wandered around working as a photographer, translator, and assorted other roles, eventually settling in

Mexico and working as an archaeologist/adventurer (with support from some private benefactors back in Europe). He appears to have published about 18 books, most about Mexico and Central America, but also the Middle East, and collections of poetry. He died on an expedition in Guatamala in 1966 at the age of 56. Secret of the Forest[3] was published (in German) in 1959, with the English translation appearing in 1963.

The book is an interesting middle-ground between an out-right travelogue and a group of archaeological surveys. What's most interesting (for me, at least) here is Cordan's detailed descriptions of the conditions by which these expeditions were mounted. As the events of the book date from sixty or so years ago, the conditions for "archeological tourism" in Central America and the Yucatan were hardly what they are today (and even today, many of these ruins can not be conveniently accessed due to the extreme conditions of the areas they're in). As is predictable for a book from a less "politically correct" age, there are a lot of blanket assertions to the "types" of various groups, from the *indios*, the *mestizos/ladinos*, to the deep-jungle Lacandons ... not so much based on any anthropological data as years of dealing with these people. However, these lend a certain color to the book, bringing scenes to life more than they might have been without.

Frankly, there is not much of an "arc" to the narrative, nor any particular point being made here. The author does make an effort to put the entire into context with the time-lines as understood then (although he does put forth material to substantively challenge some of the presently "orthodox" assumptions, including elements suggestive of the starting point of the Mayan calendar, which he figures to 3,373 bce, while not being *historically* specific, is "generally" pegged to the beginning of maize as a crop, and the establishment of settled agricultural communities in the region), as well as the peoples and cultures (and recent history) involved.

Most of the book is looking at his adventures as they unfolded, however, with details of places, individuals, challenges (especially in "expedition management" of the time), and conditions, as well as, of course, the ruins that they worked on. It seems that in the decades that Cordan was exploring the Mayan region, archaeology was turning the corner from "institutional tomb-robbing" to the science of study and preservation that it's evolved into. Cordan was definitely of the latter sort in spirit, but still of the former in the short term. He bewails what's become of the rare and fabulous artifacts he discovered (but had to leave *in situ*) that later appear plundered (and cut up) in various catalogs, yet he also gifts items to key people assisting him (as well as his European benefactors), and several times refers to a particularly excellent jade piece that his adopted son discovered that "would pay for his university".

The translation here is quite good, as the text is virtually transparent except in a couple of places (citing verse) where the German original would have been useful to be preserved, or a particular technical word might have been better left standing. I don't know if any of his other books made it into English, and if they didn't, that's quite a shame, as Secret of the Forest[4] is both enjoyable and informative, and his other titles sound interesting. It appears that all his books are out of print at this point, as Amazon only has used versions of this, and a handful of his other titles (in German) listed.

The good news is that you *can* find a copy of this if you're interested in checking it out, but you're going to have to do some digging. This was published before ISBNs were in place, so it's a matter of searching by name, and there are *six* entries on Amazon for this (strangely, *none* on BN.com), with "very good" copies available for four bucks or so (and one "like new" for fifty bucks). As noted, I'd love to see this back in print, and his other works translated, so if a look at "free-lance archaeology" from the 50's appeals to you, go grab those copies that are out there!

Notes:

1. http://btripp-books.livejournal.com/113582.html

2-4. http://amzn.to/1O8Cm9U

Monday, June 27, 2011[1]

I hear the train a'comin' ...

This is yet another of the gems I picked up at that Open Books[2] "box sale" a couple of months back. I was thrilled to find a copy, as this was one of those books lurking in my "ought to read sometime" list in the less-traveled back corridors of my mind, and running into it there made it easy and convenient, almost *imperative* given the "just throw it in with the other books" nature of that sale!

I had been *aware* of The Cluetrain Manifesto: The End of Business as Usual[3] since back in the days of Y2K hysteria ... the original web site[4] (which is still there, albeit in a dozen or so languages at this point), but it just seemed "one of those things pointing to the future" and didn't have that much of an effect on me. A collaborative effort of Rick Levine, Christopher Locke, Doc Searls, and David Weinberger, the book is an expansion of the initial "manifesto" (which only takes up 10 pages of this edition) with its "95 Theses" about how the Internet had been and would be changing communication, business, and culture. Given that this was produced a dozen years ago (an eternity in "web time"), it's impressive how well what's discussed and/or decreed in here has held up as on-target over the years. Reading it, I was frequently reminded of similar accuracy in Seth Godin's early works, which point along a very similar vector to this.

What's a "cluetrain" you ask? That's an interesting story:

> During one discussion, Doc told us about an acquaintance at a company that was free-falling out of the Fortune 500 who said "The cluetrain stopped there four times a day for ten years and no one ever took delivery." Almost before we stopped laughing, Doc told us, "I just registered the domain name 'cuetrain.com'"

The book arose from conversations along those lines ...

> Around the turn of 1999, we found ourselves talking about two closely related issues: why the media coverage of the Web was so wrong and why most businesses have their heads shoulders-high up their butts when it came to what the Web is about.

Obviously with 95 theses, I'm not going to list all of them, but they start with "1 – Markets are conversations." and end with "95 – We are waking up and linking to each other. We are watching. But we are not waiting." ... the book consists of 7 essays which expand on themes raised in the Manifesto proper, penned by a combination of the 4 authors (Weinberger has two to himself, and co-authors another two, Locke has two to himself and co-authors one with Weinberger, Levine has one to himself, and Searles is co-author on another). As is frequently the case in collaboratively authored books, the tone varies piece-to-piece as different people step to the fore, however the *focus* is reasonably consistent, making this a better read than many "group effort" books tend to be.

Probably due to The Cluetrain Manifesto[5] being centered more on *communications* than the specific modes thereof, there are less "anachronisms" than other "the web is going to change everything" books of its vintage, although what's discussed is certainly notably in a particular time frame. Here's a bit from a discussion of "Chat" (ala the classic AOL chat rooms or their predecessors in IRC):

> *Because it is immediate – taking place in realtime – chat can enable conversation that feels more genuine, more substantial, and more human than any other Net channel. ... One definition of community is a group of people who care about each other more than they have to. This isn't a business exchange, even remotely. It is conversation, the verbal glue binding people separated by geography into a community.*

This certainly puts a context around current Social Media platforms, almost defining the "special sauce" of Twitter, or what so many people find in the muddled morass of Facebook.

This is, at heart, however, a *business book* and most of the "meat" of it addresses the "cluelessness" of business-as-usual practices, especially as they relate to the new transparency and immediacy provided by the Web.

> *We have been trained throughout our business careers to suppress our individual voice and to sound like a "professional", that is, to sound like everyone else. This professional voice is distinctive. And weird. Taken out of context, it is as mannered as the ritualistic dialogue of the seventeenth-century French court. ... We may be accustomed to the professional voice, but it isn't natural, God-given or neutral: it's the voice of middle-aged white men who will do anything to keep people from seeing how frightened they are.*

Speaking as a middle-aged white man, I can attest to the fear, and the awful sense that nothing is the way "it was supposed to be" when we grew up, and I can almost sympathize with my starched-shirt peers who cling desperately to the "corporate facade" to try to preserve those things they are so worried of losing!

There is much in here as well about marketing, as that was how business first (and still) sees the Web, as a new TV to flog their messages ...

> *Of course companies and products can change their identities (and even their natures) over time. Volkswagen no longer bears (for most of us) their history stated in its very name: Hitler's car for the proud German people. ... And if a company is genuinely confused about what it is, there's an easy way to find out: listen to what your market says you are. If it's not to your liking, think long and hard before assuming that the market is wrong, composed of a lot of people who are just too dumb or blind to understand the Inner You. If you've been claiming to be the Time Company for two years but the market still thinks of you as the Overpriced Executive Trophy Watchmaker, then, sorry, but that's your position. If you don't like what you're hearing, the marketing task is not to change the market's <u>idea</u> of who you are, but <u>actually</u> to change who you are. And that can take a generation: look at Volkswagen.*

Needless to say, the MBA corps out there have only grudgingly taken any of this to heart, but it's refreshing to know that "the cluetrain" is at least trying to make deliveries at their offices.

The Cluetrain Manifesto[6] is still in print, in a 10th anniversary paperback edition, but like-new hardcover copies can be had for a penny plus shipping (that would be $4 to the newbies) from the Amazon new/used vendors. And you can even get this one *for free* as the authors have the entire text up on the site[7] if you want to take advantage of it. Whether you get it at retail, used, or free, I would recommend this as a useful thing to add to your mental files.

Notes:

1. http://btripp-books.livejournal.com/113715.html
2. http://www.open-books.org/
3. http://amzn.to/20SBSRQ
4. http://cluetrain.com/
5-6. http://amzn.to/20SBSRQ
7. http://cluetrain.com/book/

Saturday, July 9, 2011[1]

What we're made of ...

I've been on a bit of a run with "wins" via Library-Thing.Com[2]'s "Early Reviewer" program, having being awarded a book a month over the past several months by the LTER's "Almighty Algorithm". This is the latest (well, strictly speaking, not, as I'm awaiting the arrival of June's win, this one's from the May batch) from them. I was somewhat surprised that they matched this up with my library, as although I've read a lot of science books in the past, I've not done many recently, and very little of that was in the *biological* sciences.

I really didn't have any solid preconceptions of what John Quackenbush's The Human Genome: Book of Essential Knowledge[3] would be like, although the description was a good bit more in-depth than is usual for the blurbs on the monthly LTER offering page. While I can't really speak to how "essential" the material in this "book of essential knowledge" is, the author certainly makes an effort to cover a wide range of subjects that are concerned with the Human Genome Project, and in doing so sacrifices depth for breadth in this compact 176-page volume.

The book begins with politics, relating the 2000 press conference jointly held by Bill Clinton and Tony Blair, announcing the "completion" of the genetic map, although large portions of the genome had not been addressed at that point, and work is still continuing. The Human Genome Project was a government project, started in 1990, which later found itself in competition with the private company Celera. Fortunately, to a certain extent, these two entities worked cooperatively, although with different source DNA.

Quackenbush then sets the stage for the project by going back to the earliest days of genetic research, with Mendel, Darwin, the development of Cell Theory, and progressive improvements on how we were able to explore these zones, leading up to the discovery of DNA and the early efforts of gene sequencing. He then tracks the progression of creatures used to study genes, from bacteria (with a couple of million "base pairs"), to yeast (13 million base pairs), to roundworms (100 million base pairs), fruit flies (the familiar *Drosophila* of highschool biology classes, at 130 million base pairs), and eventually to Human genome, with 3 *billion* base pairs. The number of "base pairs" of nucleotides does not, however, dictate the number of *genes*, as human DNA has about 25,000 genes, not vastly more than the roundworm's 20,000. In fact, many *plants* have many more genes, with far fewer base pairs, the poplar tree, for example, has only 550,000 base pairs (less than 2% of humans') but nearly twice the genes, at 45,000 (the reason for this is supposed to be the "rootedness" of plants, which can't move away from unfavorable environmental factors, so need to "carry" their options with them).

The next factor looks at how genes are *expressed* (many other factors strongly effect how a particular gene will perform), how mutation figures in, and how genetics distribute across populations. Much of the genetic heritage is common to *all* life on the planet, going up to as much as a 98% commonality with the chimpanzees. Within humanity, there is only about 1/10th of 1% variation between any two people, which, conveniently, means that the two genome maps being worked on will provide a very good approximation of the genes across the entire population.

From here the book turns to disease, first with a full chapter looking at various types of cancer, and how genes may or may not have influence in its development. This is followed by another chapter that looks at many diseases, a number of which have been determined to arise from specific genetic factors. Here the book shifts gears again and takes a look at what the genome can tell us about evolution, both in general (arising from the simplest forms and on towards more complex creatures), and in tracing humanity's origins and complicated movements from its African roots in spreading across the planet. Finally, "the future" is looked at, with projections on what continuing knowledge of the genome might bring, from the dystopian scenarios familiar from science fiction, into "personal medicine" based on one's individual genetic make-up.

Now, The Human Genome[4] is pitched as aimed at the "general reader", but I have to note that this came close to "losing" me at a few points. The author is trying to get so much information, in so many different areas, into the book, that he, at times, apparently leaves out explanatory material that would make things clearer. Of course, the good side of that is that he's having to move on to the next subject so quickly that there's not much opportunity to get overly "bogged down". I did want to make a note of this, however, as I *am* a "science reader", and would expect to *not* have these difficulties!

Both B&N and Amazon have this at about a third off of (the very reasonable) cover price, but this should (being out for just a few months) be at the brick-and-mortar places too. It's one of those books that I'm glad *to have read*, although it didn't necessarily engage me cover-to-cover. If you're interested in genetic research, however, you should definitely pick up a copy!

Notes:

1. http://btripp-books.livejournal.com/114053.html
2. http://www.librarything.com/catalog/BTRIPP
3-4. http://amzn.to/1mzcwWd

Sunday, July 10, 2011[1]

The way these should have been ...

Well ... some times you wish for something and it comes to pass. Of course, James Redfield's The Celestine Vision: Living the New Spiritual Awareness[2] has been out for 14 years, so I might have sought it out before now, but this is the book that I kept saying he *ought to* write, rather than his consistently frustrating "novels". As regular readers of this space know, I spent a goodly amount of the 80's studying shamanism, with a couple of notable trips down to Peru. When *The Celestine Prophecy* came out in 1993, I had a number of people recommend it to me for the Peruvian elements in it. I found reading that an exercise in irritation as he had scenes in that which were *so* wrong that he might as well have been saying that the Eiffel Tower was in *London*, but then he'd follow up that section with a very cogent presentation of high-level Incan shamanic exercises! Over the years, I came to realize that his "novels" were simply his attempt to "pill the cat", as it were, stuffing bits of truly esoteric knowledge into a matrix of "popular" fiction like one might attempt to hide a pill in chopped liver to get it into one's feline companion. Every time I read one of his awkward, wooden, shallow "novels" I'd think *"why doesn't he just write this stuff out?"* without the trappings of an adventure story. Well, The Celestine Vision[3] is pretty much that book.

I do, however, wish that he'd *update* this, as there have been materials in his later two books which don't appear in here, and I'd *really* like to know, if not his *sources*, the more straight-forward presentation of the information! This was preceded by two "experiential guides", and the sense I get from this is that it arises out of running "Celestine workshops", and needing to have a non-fiction based resource for the folks attending those.

I'm always happy when a New Age book presents a solid, cohesive, and reasonably focused exposition of a spiritual path, and this (to a greater or lesser extent) does that. Spread out over a dozen chapters, this is a collection of sub-sections ranging from 1-3 pages, a format that prevents *too* much wandering off into "woo woo", and so keeps the book well on track. The chapter titles give a fairly good idea of where the book goes, so here they are: Early Intuitions; Experiencing the Coincidences; Understanding Where We Are; Entering the Responsive Universe; Overcoming the Power Struggle; Experiencing the Mystical; Discovering Who We Are; Evolving Consciously; Living the New Interpersonal Ethic; Moving toward a Spiritual Culture; The View from the Afterlife; and Visualizing Human Destiny.

The book brings in lots of pieces, there are "law of attraction" sorts of things which are likely to owe more to the Napoleon Hill era books than to the more recent manifestations, there are inter-personal dynamic bits that, while framed in "energy" work, seem likewise sourced from psychology, numerous university-based psi experiments are described (if not outright referenced), and there is a lot of material about energy and different levels of being that certainly have resonance with significant shamanic and mystical traditions with which I'm familiar. This bit is for those working with "intention", and could be applied in various settings:

> *One group of studies showed something else that is especially interesting. Though our ability to affect the world works in both cases, nondirective intention (that is, holding the idea that the <u>very best</u> should happen without injecting our opinion) works better than directive intention (holding the idea that a specific outcome should occur). This seems to indicate that there is a principle or law built into our connectedness with the rest of the universe that keeps our egos in check.*

The techniques presented here are almost always brought around to "practical" applications, from "finding the best seat" in a room to allow for synchronistic encounters to happen, to ways to best manage group and relationship dynamics, and even proposals for "tithing" economies.

Needless to say, this was a very pleasant surprise when stacked up against his other books, and I would recommend it to anybody interested in "new-agey" things. Obviously, this caveat comes into play because The Celestine Vision[4] *is* in the "woo woo" stream of the novels, but the material is reasonably presented here, and even is written in a far more amenable style that anything else I've read of his.

Both Amazon and B&N have this at about 1/3rd off of cover, but I was able to snag my copy from the new/used guys who currently have "very good" copies of even the hardcover (I got the paperback) for as little as a penny (plus shipping). If this sounds like something that would appeal to you, I'd definitely recommend picking up one of those!

Notes:

1. http://btripp-books.livejournal.com/114394.html

2-4. http://amzn.to/1O8B9PR

Saturday, July 16, 2011[1]

Tibet is Tibet is Tibet ...

Slowly but surely making it through my part of that last Open Books[2] box sale ... this is the latest of those that I've gotten to. As usual with things purchased in the random acquisitional frenzy that those sales engender, I did not come to this book with much intention ... it looked interesting, sounded like something I'd like to read, so it went into the box ... as such, I didn't have much expectation of what it was about. Lee Feigon's Demystifying Tibet: Unlocking the Secrets of the Land of the Snows[3] could have exhibited a wide range of themes, given that title/subtitle pairing, but if you wanted to sum the book up in a sentence it would be something along the lines of *"Tibet's not part of China ... no, really"*. While I'm certainly among the "choir" to whom he's "preaching" on this point, I kept having the "OK, we get *that*, when do get to the secrets and the demystifying?" reaction, pretty much at the end of each chapter.

I don't suppose that naming this *"A Cultural Survey of Tibet"* would have sold as well as a book dealing with "secrets" and mysteries, but it would have been a far more *accurate* title. Frankly, it is quite a *satisfying* look at the history of Tibet and the cultural development of the Tibetan people, which starts *fifty million years ago* when the land that is presently at altitudes over 11,000ft was a coastal plain on a long-drained ocean ... and runs the narrative up to its 1996 publication date. There's anthropology here, there's sociology here, there's politics here, and there's certainly history in various forms (art, religion, military, etc.) here, but nearly no "mystery" nor "secrets".

Again, the thrust appears to establish the *difference* of the Tibetans from the surrounding peoples, and especially the Chinese at each step here. From architecture, linguistic forms, written language (Tibetan is written in an alphabet based on Sanskrit, rather than in ideograms of Chinese), art and costume, and on into the idiosyncratic religious form of Vajrayana Buddhism, each section of the first part of the book works to establish the separateness of the Tibetans.

Although being generally conversant on the subject of Tibet's history, I found that Demystifying Tibet[4] provided an interesting read into the ebb and flow of various cultural influences between Tibet and its neighbors. At times it was closely allied with particular dynasties, at others in bitter struggles. Tibet was obviously strongly influenced by the outside (such as when Buddhism established itself there and eventually largely absorbed the native shamanistic Bön religion), but still maintained an identifiable "national identity". Much of this, of course, can be attributed to Tibet's geography, ringed by the world's highest mountain ranges, it required a focused effort to *get* there in the days before aircraft (and, at those altitudes, it's still not trivial), so there was far less opportunity for cultural intermixing compared to almost anywhere else.

The most fascinating part of this is the later *political* history, starting in the mid-1700's with assorted relations with the Qing dynasty, moving into Tibet's role as both a buffer zone and something of a "pawn" in The Great Game (standing in the middle of British India, Russia, and the then-isolationist Qing Chinese), on through the wars of the early part of the last century, and the rise of Chinese communism. Obviously, for theocratic Tibet, the rise of belligerent, expansionistic, and aggressively atheist Red China was a Very Bad Thing, as the "new neighbors" had both a massive army and a habit of conflating monasteries living off of donated peasant labor with "feudal abuse of workers" … and the grim recent history is spun out in very informative detail.

One of the most fascinating points that Feigon makes here is that the Chinese "national myth" (of Han superiority over all other Asian races, etc., and having had borders encompassing any region that had ever even been in "formalized trading" arrangements with previous Imperial dynasties) is perceived as being rather fragile, and is more and more challenged by things like Tibetan freedom movements globally, and the likes of the Tiananmen Square protests domestically. He paints this as an intentionally promulgated fantasy aimed at maintaining centralized control by the communist government over such a vast and culturally heterogenous national entity. He provides many instances where the "myth" of Tibet being "part of China" has not squared with the actions of the Chinese:

> The Chinese have not been forthcoming about exactly how good a deal they offered the Tibetans. To this day the Chinese argue that the acceptance of this agreement marked the official Tibetan acknowledgment that Tibet is and always has been part of China. But the very existence of the Seventeen-Point Agreement clearly shows that this is not the case and indicates that in the 1950s the Chinese viewed the region as distinct from the rest of China.
>
> For one thing, China did not sign such agreements with other areas it "liberated". Only in Tibet did China acknowledge that it was dealing with a political, cultural, social, and ethical system so different from its own that China needed to guarantee Tibet's political and religious autonomy. The existence of the agreement indicates the Chinese recognized Tibet as a separate and independent ethnic area that deserved different treatment from the rest of the country. Tibet was not an integral part of China but an area with special status.

So ... if you're looking for a detailed cultural history of Tibet, half old and half new, this is a great book for you. If you're looking to "take a peek behind the curtain" and find Shambhala, you're gong to be disappointed. Fortunately, I (as noted above) hit this without any particular preconceptions, so found it quite to my liking.

Demystifying Tibet[5] appears to be still in print in a paperback edition, but "very good" copies of the hardcover can be had for as little as 15¢ (plus shipping). Even if you've read a lot about Tibet, I think you'll find this a useful "cultural study", and it would certainly be an informative place to start if one was just now looking into "The Land of Snows".

Notes:

1. http://btripp-books.livejournal.com/114641.html

2. http://www.open-books.org/

3-5. http://amzn.to/20SAy1k

Sunday, July 17, 2011[1]

Sure as Kilimanjaro rises like Olympus above the Serengeti ...

This is a rare one in that I actually made a point of requesting a review copy (from the good folks at Wiley), after seeing it referenced in my Twitter stream. It is also one of the first books that I've had a "first encounter" with via its *own* Twitter account, which had a post re-tweeted by an account I follow, leading me to send the e-mail. This might have not caught my eye as much were I not still penning The Job Stalker[2] blog over on the Tribune's "ChicagoNow" site ... it did, however, seem the sort of thing that my readers there might find of interest, as those have been few and far between of late in what I've been reading.

I did *not* anticipate getting through this as quickly as I did ... two long El rides and a couple of waits for a bus pretty much covered it, and I had it ready to review a mere 24 hours after its arrival. This is, generally speaking, A Good Thing, as it means that Stefan Swanepoel's Surviving Your Serengeti: 7 Skills to Master Business and Life[3] wasn't "a struggle" to get through, usually indicating it being both engaging and reasonably well written. This is not to say it's a classic, or that I didn't have some caveats going in on it.

I must admit, before I requested a copy, I did "a bad thing" and went to read some of the reviews that are already out there (the book is fairly new, having just come out this March) on it. This typically "sets one up" on how one's going to be "seeing" the book, but I wanted to get a sense of if it was going to be worth it (for either Wiley or me) to get a copy ... and some of these were *brutal*. I was, needless to say, quite relieved to find that the book was no where near "as bad" as some were painting it, but, in retrospect, I can see some of the points raised.

First of all this is a "fiction" with characters representing others in adjusted scenarios (the protagonist and the author both have been married 30 years and have two kids, but the former has girls and the latter boys), and one always comes to wonder where the line runs between "personal experience" and fictionalized elements. In this it reminds me a bit of James Redfield's *Celestine* novels, and approaches the territory staked out by Marlo Morgan in *Mutant Message: Down Under*, although not representing itself as that sort of "native wisdom". Frankly, I was surprised to find that the author hailed from Kenya, so much of the material here could well have been absorbed first-hand in his youth. However, this presents "7 Skills to Master Business and Life", and doing so in this sort of context reminded me quite a lot of Mark Victor Hansen & Robert G. Allen's books *Cash in a Flash: Fast Money in Slow Times* and *The One Minute Millionaire: The Enlightened Way to Wealth*, where half of the book (oddly, in those cases, every other page) is a story about how a group of characters came to discover and use the processes detailed in the rest of the book.

Surviving Your Serengeti[4] also had the possibility of wandering off into insufferable "newageism" of the "what sort of an animal are *you*?" variety, but I was pleased to find that Swanepoel managed to present what *is* that sort of a structure in a very reasonable and applicable way.

The "7 skills" are all related to the behaviors of certain animals that the protagonist and his wife encounter when on a Safari trip that she'd won in a contest. The set-up and descriptions of these folks' lives and situations could have been cribbed right out of those Hansen/Allen books, but they at least provided some context and texture to the characters (as opposed to Redfield's wooden portrayals). The scenarios are fairly contrived, but at least are plausible within the supporting story arc (which does unfortunately remind one of a *Celestine* book) and allows for a fairly diverse group of animals to be introduced in the narrative.

To cut to the chase, here's the line-up: "The Enduring Wildebeest", "The Strategic Lion", "The Enterprising Crocodile", "The Efficient Cheetah", "The Graceful Giraffe", "The Risk-Taking Mongoose", and "The Communicating Elephant". In each case, the protagonist is introduced to these animals in the wild where he can observe their behaviors, and these "skills" are discussed within the context of those actions. Each is dealt with in a separate chapter, and at the end of these there is a section which (quite usefully) takes the "skill" out of the animal context and suggests ways that this could be used in business, at home, or (the reason I sought out the book in the first place) the job hunt.

Part of the story deals with figuring out "which of the animals you are", which is probably something that I wouldn't have applied much attention to, but they have provided a handy on-line quiz that will help you narrow that down (at http://whatanimalami.com/[5]) ... which determined that I was a Wildebeest (and I thought I only *smelled* that way!).

Surviving Your Serengeti[6] is no big life-changer, but a light reminder of where you can find examples to use in your daily activities, framed within the animal world, but re-focused as a template for personal action. As noted, this is pretty much brand new, so it should be available at your local brick-and-mortar booksellers, but the on-line guys both have it at about 40% off and there *are* already copies in the used channels. Again, this is a *much* better book than it might have been (given the caveats of things it resembles on various levels), and has been unfairly slammed in other contexts. If you're interested in a quick-reading story about an African Safari, with a lot of attention paid to animals and their activities, with take-aways you can use in your life, do consider picking up a copy ... I liked it well enough, and certainly enjoyed the read!

Notes:
1. http://btripp-books.livejournal.com/114832.html
2. http://jobstalker.info/
3-4. http://amzn.to/1RA3UeW
5. http://whatanimalami.com/
6. http://amzn.to/1RA3UeW

Saturday, July 30, 2011[1]

He asked, while shoving the Nunchuks under his jacket ...

Well, I'm *almost* done with the haul I made at the last "box sale" over at Open Books[2], this being one of those. As I've previously noted, I'm no great fan of "business books", and, frankly, had never read *any* prior to my '96-'97 job search. I have, however, somewhat gotten into the habit, when I see something that seems "interesting" and has the potential to plug a gap in my general business knowledge.

What Sticks: Why Most Advertising Fails and How to Guarantee Yours Succeeds[3] by Rex Briggs & Greg Stuart is one of those books that teeters on the edge of being a long-format promotional piece for the authors' company, as it presents *everything* in context of how it did work or would work within their proprietary approach (much like How Companies Win[4], reviewed here a few months back). The over-all system is called C.O.P. (and, notably, the acronym has *never* become lucid to me, and I've had to look it up over a dozen times now) for "Communication Optimization Process".

The key "hook" to the book is here:

> There's an old quote in advertising ... "I know half my advertising is wasted; I'm just not sure which half." In our own research based on careful quantitative analysis, we found that the actual waste is about one-third {$112 billion} of the nearly $300 billion advertising spend in the United States. More startling is that 19 percent of advertising fails outright and another 67 percent could achieve significant improvement that would require no additional spending

Obviously, those numbers are attention-getting and the authors show how their system can achieve those improvements. They advocate a series of meetings, first to set up a "shared definition of success", then cover "scenario planning", and then get into the specifics of what to do when. These are set up as "the 4Ms": Motivations, Message, Media, and Maximization. Perhaps the key element is understanding consumer motivations. The authors keep returning to the point that the consumer is looking at the ad in a completely different mid-set than the marketer or agency. The consumer is very likely in a low-attention state and giving only peripheral focus to the ad, this in contrast to the client paying for the ad or the agency creating the ad, where every fine detail is considered at length. On thing that is pointed out here is that it is pretty much *impossible* for the folks *producing* the ads to achieve anything *near* the "innocence" of the consumer's state when approaching the ad, but they offer up ways of analyzing how meaning comes through. Motivation can have a rational, physical, emotional, status, time, and/or "fictional" base, and it's essential that one's messages hit the right motivation buttons.

One of the more fascinating parts of What Sticks[5] are the central chapters of Part III, but they're a bit technical to cover in this review, however they are: "Messaging and the Transformation from Intuition to Science", "Messaging Across Consumer Touchpoints", "Media Mechanics: *Media Allocations's "Law of Physics"*", Media Psychologics: *How Meaning is Created Through Media Strategies*", and Media Optimization: *Getting More Bang for Your Buck*". This book came out in 2006, and it's interesting how *dated* much of the discussion of moving parts of marketing budgets over to the Internet sounds just five years down the road ... in here it's presented as almost "daring", and deals a lot with buying big chunks of AOL's real estate! However, they show cases from major marketers who improved the over-all performance (by 14%, for instance) of their campaigns by "tweaking" the impression figures for TV and Print ads and shifting those dollars into Internet buys (in this example, pulling down TV from 6.0 to 5.5 impressions, and print from 2.6 to 2 ... where much of that extra was non-productive anyway ... which allowed Internet reach to go from 10% to 60%, with *the same dollars*.

A final thing that caught my eye was the 70/20/10 "allocation" formula, with 70% of your dollars going to the stuff that you know is going to work for you, 20% of your dollars going to "innovative" approaches, and 10% being tagged for "disruptive" innovations. They compare this with Google's famed 20% of staff time being set aside for things that *the employees* want to work on, outside of their assigned tasks. Obviously, having more of *this* kind of thinking moving through the corporate world is A Good Thing!

What Sticks[6] appears to still be in print, so is likely to be at your local full-service (those with business books) book monger, The on-line guys, however, have it at about 30% off of cover and the used vendors have "good" copies of the hardcover for as little as a penny (plus shipping, of course). So, if this sounds interesting to you (and some more info is at http://whatsticks.net[7]) you might want to pick up a copy.

Notes:

1. http://btripp-books.livejournal.com/115446.html

2. http://www.open-books.org/

3. http://amzn.to/1mz9x05

4. http://btripp-books.livejournal.com/110397.html

5-6. http://amzn.to/1mz9x05

7. http://whatsticks.net/

Sunday, July 31, 2011[1]

None dare call it "seedy" ...

I recently was in touch with the Wiley folks about another book, and they offered to send out four new ones, including this. I'd noted (maybe over in The Job Stalker[2]) that I'd not had much to write about book-wise on the job search, and this set certainly puts me on the other side of that!

Admittedly, Jon Gordon's The Seed: Finding Purpose and Happiness in Life and Work[3] is not about the job search, but more about "getting one's head together" in general. As I've mentioned here before, I'm not a great fan of "teaching stories" or other "fictionalized" accounts, so moving into this ran smack into that attitude. There obviously *must* be an audience out there that *likes* to have its metaphysical info packaged this way, given what massive successes various books in the genre have been, but I'm always struggling with them, trying to anticipate what the *point* is that the author's dancing around, or cringing in anticipation of some (to me) less savory turn of plot.

As these sorts of books go, however, this was OK ... while the main character *had* come out of a "preachy" background (it's a standard modality in the genre, I'm afraid), and had *considered* Bible-thumping as a career, that was pretty much as far as it went into being a "tract", as in most of the rest of the book whenever the "G-word" came up it was fairly solidly presented in a non-denominational theistic mode. This is, of course, one of my main problems with these "teaching stories", I spend the whole book steeling myself to deflect the "preaching" that is typically snuck in ... like going to lunch with a network marketer, you're getting twitchy in anticipation of when "the pitch" is going to come. While that shoe never quite drops in The Seed[4], it does constantly feel like it's "just around the corner". Of course, that could "just be me" ... but if you have the same hesitancy with this sort of thing, it's good to know going in!

Of course, the other problem with story books like this is that they're far more difficult to sum up than books that say what they have to say in a coherent and direct manner. This is about a guy named Josh who had grown up in the ministry, had been some sort of singing youth pastor before going to college, discovered that business was more to his liking than preaching, and had gone off to make a fairly good start to a career in some company that is only vaguely fleshed out. After 5 years there he is somewhat burned out, and his boss orders him off on a 2-week vacation to decide if he wants to stay there. This is where the book starts, him driving off to a "corn maze" to spend a day with some of his friends. Again, this is one of the things I "have issues with" in these sorts of books, just as the job isn't defined, "his friends" seem to only exist to get him to "where he needs to be" for the story points. I guess at this point, for the fiction fans out there, I should throw up a big >SPOILER WARNING< ... as what he encounters in the corn maze is a suddenly-appearing old farmer (who is, as is no great surprise, a ghost) who talks to him about his life path and hands him a seed, along with a bunch of discussion and instructions regarding it that Josh (ahem ...) *somehow* manages to retain verbatim the rest of the book.

Once out of the maze, he is convinced to go up in a plane ride, which very conveniently is right there by the corn maze and has a pilot who's eager to take up one more rider (*and* his dog), for another dose of unexpected "wisdom" that just so happens to neatly dove-tail with the words of the Farmer. Oh, did I mention the dog ... his dog is called Dharma, a gift to him of his now-departed college girlfriend, and he spends a lot of time talking through his thoughts to the dog, who then *adds her own commentary* about how "humans are" and how she knows stuff that he still has to work out.

He ends up encountering various other "convenient" connections, from a restaurant manager that he used to work for (who unexpectedly just happens to need some staff *just when he shows up*), to a head-hunter who calls him to immediately fly out to an interview for a very attractive job. He has encounters with his favorite professor from college, a student in a wheelchair who used to be a football player, a fellow in an airplane, and another couple of visits to the farm.

About three quarters through the book, he comes to the conclusion that he'll go back (refreshed and refocused) to his old job. His boss it thrilled, and he starts moving forward. At this point the book sort of telescopes through time showing Josh using the principles he'd learned in his 2-week assigned vacation to developing his career. To check out some of this, you can go to the "teleseminar" at http://seed11.com[5] ... but you can also just flip to p.144 where the main points of the book are presented.

Needless to say, The Seed[6] was not in the most useful format for me (I probably got more out of P.144 than the rest of the book!), but if "stories" like this speak to you, I'm sure you'll find it instructive. Again, this was not "bad", just "not my cup of tea", and I was pleased that it had ghostly apparitions and (almost) talking dogs instead of the preachy stuff that I kept expecting when the author gets into flinging the G-word around as much as he does at some points. This has only been out a month or so, and should be at your local brick-and-mortar, but both of the on-line guys currently have it at a 44% discount.

Notes:

1. http://btripp-books.livejournal.com/115648.html

2. http://jobstalker.info/

3-4. http://amzn.to/1mz8ZHn

5. http://seed11.com/

6. http://amzn.to/1mz8ZHn

Wednesday, August 3, 2011[1]

Star light, star bright ...

I must admit that I am a HUGE fan of this genre ... and have read a number of other books by its authors and their assorted other associates. It is frustrating that, given the attention and fieldwork involved in this quest, more material remnants have not come to light.

Keeper of Genesis: A Quest for the Hidden Legacy of Mankind[2] is by Robert Bauval and Graham Hancock, being yet another look at the peculiarities of the Giza Plateau in Egypt. Bauval and Hancock (with others, such as John Anthony West) promote a belief that there was an ancient "root civilization" which both preceded and *seeded* the historical ancient cultures which arose in the past few thousand years. West (not involved in this project), has traveled over the world and compared the massive buildings, with mortarless finely-set huge stones, and it is with these sorts of examples that Bauval (an engineer by training) starts asking questions ... as the *older* monuments (such as the "Sphinx Temple") have megalithic construction featuring stones weighing from 50 to *200* tons apiece ... stones that we would be hard-pressed to even MOVE without the most powerful lifting technology developed. In addition to those issues, there's the weathering of the stone within the Sphinx enclosure, famously studied by Boston University geologist Robert Schoch, and by others since. By their determination the Sphinx enclosure had to have been carved out in a time when the weather in Egypt was *much* wetter, with an estimate of prior to 10,000 BC. Standard Egyptologists hold that everything at Giza dates only to about 2,500 BC, and consider any other projections "pure fantasy", however they do not have the technical specialization for either the engineering questions nor the geological questions, and, frankly, the data that much of the dating is based on is very flimsy.

Most of this book, however, is based on astronomical considerations. Current "sky map" programs allow researchers to run time forward and backwards connecting to various observation points on Earth. The alignment of the stars in the constellation of Orion (representing Osiris to the Egyptians) has been mapped with remarkable precision to the area of Giza, with the 3 large pyramids falling in alignment with the stars in "Orion's belt". However, the specific alignments that the stars-to-Giza mappings are for a time, again, far before the "official" dating of the area, including the placement of the Sphinx, which is aligned to a point on the horizon which would have been the Sun rising in Leo (in the "age of Leo", like the "age of Pisces" giving way to the "age of Aquarius" now), in approximately 10,500 BC.

Other aspects come into play as well, like the "shafts" coming out of the "King's Chamber" which led to the discovery of the *hidden* shafts that explorers found in the "Queen's Chamber" by punching through the stone walls. These shafts also point to key stars, stars whose cultic significance goes back to some of the earliest Egyptian documents, preserved as astrological texts inscribed in sarcophagi and tombs. The argument that Bauval and Hancock come up with is that while the major pyramids were *built* approximately 3,000 BC, they were sited on a far earlier plan, and constructed with processes that we still can't satisfactorily figure out (aside from things like their remarkably precise orientations, sixty times more accurate than what could be expected from any "by sight" measuring, the most "popular" suggestions for schemes of moving the blocks into place would have required ramps involving many times more material than what is *in* the pyramids, with no sign of any such *massive* earth moving having been done there). This implies that there was an advanced culture of which the ancient Egyptians were a *survival*.

Of course, no "incontrovertible" evidence of any such civilization has been discovered, although there are tantalizing pointers towards such in the more ancient monuments of many regions on the planet, where massive constructions were achieved with megalithic blocks, finely hewn, and set precisely without mortar in ages when most of humanity was, by "official" timelines, barely out of the stone age. As the authors repeatedly return to, there are *facts* about Giza which are there to be measured, facts that are hard to dismiss if they are taken on their own terms (moving a 200 ton block with Bronze Age technology, for example, or aligning a 13-acre monument with precision that would require a laser theodolite with "atomic clock" accuracy), despite how willingly they are dismissed by Egyptologists with no experience in engineering, surveying, or even religion.

The difficulty is, clearly, that this can very quickly descend into either "Space Aliens" or "Atlantis" territory. Indeed, much of what is discussed here keeps returning to work that A.R.E. (the Edgar Cayce group) has spearheaded around the Sphinx (which featured prominently in his "prophecies" regarding Atlantis), and it's hard *not* to drift off into Zechariah Sitchin-esque considerations of "outside influences" having a hand in developing early human cultures (or, early humans themselves) when looking at the technological advancement that would be required to create what's sitting there at Giza ... one of the things that Egyptologists such as Zahi Hawass claims to be "racist" as it suggests that the people of Egypt/Africa could not have *possibly* achieved these things on their own.

It appears that Keeper of Genesis[3] is currently out of print (which seems odd to me, given how related material is so frequently featured on the History Channel, etc.), but used copies are available ... I got mine via Amazon's new/used vendor listings, and "mass market paperbacks" (like what I got) are there for as little a 1¢ (plus $3.99 shipping) in "good" condition. This wasn't my favorite book in this genre, or by its authors, but it was certainly a fascinating (if frustrating in parts) read, and I'd recommend it to anybody interested in these outer fringes of historical research.

Notes:

1. http://btripp-books.livejournal.com/115962.html
2-3. http://amzn.to/20SxYZ3

Saturday, August 20, 2011[1]

80 things you should know ...

This title came to me via the LibraryThing.com "early reviewers" program, but, given that it's from Wiley, I might have been seeing a copy eventually (as they're very generous with sending me books to review). I've had a lot of success of late with the LTER, "winning" books almost every month this year, but many of those books have been disappointments, or worse. This one, however, was interesting, engaging, and even *useful* (as witnessed by the dozen or so slips of paper bookmarking things I need to get back to in it), and I'm a lot more enthusiastic about Patrick Schwerdtfeger's Marketing Shortcuts for the Self-Employed: Leverage Resources, Establish Online Credibility and Crush Your Competition[2] than I have been about anything from that program in quite a long while.

However, I find that this is an update of a previous book (2009's *Webify Your Business, Internet Marketing Secrets for the Self-Employed*), which always confuses me ... was the first book *wrong*? Has it become outdated in two years? Why the new manifestation? The difference in the titles also leads me to the one "caveat" that I have for the book ... the focus is odd, and "Webify Your Business" is a lot more accurate for most of this than "Marketing Shortcuts for the Self-Employed". I don't know what the author's specific vision is of the "self-employed" audience he's writing for, but it seems to be more along the lines of a pizza parlor or beauty salon than a writer, a coder, a graphic artist, etc. which would come to my mind when encountering that phrase ... and a lot of this falls "on the other side of that fence" for me. This is not to say that the material in the book isn't VERY handy and to the point, it's just occasionally apples to the oranges that somebody (like myself) is dealing with!

One of the best things about the book is its structure ... its 250 pages are broken into 7 sections comprising 80 chapters, with each chapter closing with a half a dozen to a dozen "action points" in a checklist. Needless to say, this forces the author into being to-the-point on each of these (having only an average of 3 pages to work with on any topic). The book is another "soup to nuts" presentation (somewhat like Joel Comm's KaChing[3]) which takes the reader through an entire arc of business activities, with the sections here being "Define Your Business Model", "Plan Your Internet Presence", "Build Your Website and Blog", "Populate Internet Properties", "Attract Qualified Prospects", and "Leverage Social Media". Again, those sure sound more like "webifying" one's business than offering "marketing shortcuts" ... but that's a quibble, not really a complaint!

To give you some idea of what I ended up bookmarking, he had resources for Market Research with which I was unfamiliar, "expanding the frame" -

which he has defined as intentionally adding higher-priced items to one's web offerings, improving your SEO "page rank" with inbound links from an array of sites set up on various platforms, a number of SEO diagnostic tools that I'd not encountered, some tricks on interpreting analytic data, a few ideas about event marketing (that I've already taken action on for one of my consulting clients), and several things to use with LinkedIn that I wasn't aware of. All of these are very helpful *to me* and I'm not (as noted) in the "sweet spot" of what I'm assuming is his target audience.

This, of course, brings me back to the *problem* I have with the book … it keeps drifting from being for "the self-employed" and back into (the previous version's) "your business" … and this is evident right off the bat. In Chapter 2 – Develop Expertise, he has this somewhat less than helpful (especially in a book of "shortcuts"!) to-do list:

1. Pick a narrow specific topic.
2. Acquire massive expertise.
3. Present yourself as an expert.

Is it just me, or doesn't step #2 there sort of imply a decade or more of working on something? Essentially everything else in the book is based on completing this three-step process … and I sure can't see any work-around on that second point. THEN, as quickly as Chapter 4 - "Problems + PAIN = Profits", the first two items of the action check list are:

- Identify the problem your product solves.
- Describe the *pain* caused by the problem.

Uh … product? What product? And, frankly, what *pain*? Last night I had a client ask me to re-work a page on his website that he'd been trying to set up using the WYSIWYG editor on the Ning platform. Obviously, his "pain" was that he wasn't able to get it to look the way he wanted it (he was pretty frustrated when he contacted me), but is my "product" knowing a bit more HTML, CSS, etc. than he does? That's a mighty slippery "product" to be pitching (especially as coding is a secondary skill set for me, and I'm not a "Ninja/Rockstar/Guru" web guy). I've encountered this concept of "pain" in other books, but I've always had a hard time wrapping it around my situation as a basis of marketing.

Again, this may be me wearing my "editor hat" here and wishing that Schwerdtfeger had started with a clean slate here for addressing the marketing concerns of the "self employed", but it was a point of recurring dissonance as I went through the book, and figured that others who are in the "knowledge worker" fields might have a similar difficulty figuring out what "their product" might be in this context.

Anyway, don't let these minor gripes take away from my over-all enthusiasm for Marketing Shortcuts for the Self-Employed[4], it's sufficiently jam-packed with both top-notch info and practical action lists that I'm convinced that anybody who's looking to expand their marketability would benefit from picking up a copy. This has just been out a couple of months at this point, so is likely available at your local brick-and-mortar book vendor which carries business books, but the on-line guys currently have it at 35% off of cover, which is probably the best deal you'll find on it (heck, even used copies of Schwerdtfeger's previous book are going for more than that!). Highly recommended.

Notes:

1. http://btripp-books.livejournal.com/116197.html
2. http://amzn.to/1mz82it
3. http://btripp-books.livejournal.com/96293.html
4. http://amzn.to/1mz82it

Sunday, August 21, 2011[1]

The early Yeats ...

This is yet another of those books picked up at the Open Books[2] "box sale" some months back ... I don't know exactly what prompted me to add it to my stack, except, of course, the flat-fee per box which ended up disengaging most of the filters that would be in place even with deeply discounted books!

Of course, having been an English major (among others) in college, I'd encountered Yeats in various settings, but as the years have gone on I've come to realize how "not deep" (to avoid calling it "shallow") one's exposure to the literature is even in top-notch Liberal Arts programs, and I've attempted to plug in missing bits as they've come up.

The current volume is W. B. Yeats: Selected Poems[3] (even though my copy has "William Butler Yeats" spelled out on its dust jacket and spine), although from reading other reviewers' snipes, I guess it should more accurately be called "the early poems" as it seems that his later, better, more popular material did not make it into this volume, for whatever reason (much to some critics' irritation).

Perhaps this is why I didn't really get particularly enthusiastic for anything in here ... it's quite a mish-mash of styles and voices, subjects and formats, ranging from 6-line barbs *at a bird* for reminding him of some lost love, to 12-page rambling retellings of Irish cultural myths, to broadsides against deadbeat would-be sponsors. It *does*, however, include one of his more famous poems, *September 1913*, which is of his political oeuvre.

Yeats was also deeply involved with Theosophy and the Golden Dawn, but (as conversant as I am on those subjects) that influence does not seem to come through much in this collection, as the places where he *does* get "mystical" are primarily in "Celtic myth" poems, almost *all* of which here are pulled back to some sort of Christian framing by the end of the piece, or have it end up being more about lost love.

That's another point here ... the first part of the book all seems to be about loss and sorrow, scarcely a poem goes without some mention of heavy sighs over things that might have been ... I don't know if that's from "callow youth" or the stylistic form he was emulating at the time.

Of course, my tastes in these things are fairly constrained to a few general streams, and I might just being cranky here, but this particular collection didn't do much for me, but you might find it far more interesting. He kept almost getting me into a particular piece, only to run off into something that was not to my liking ... quite frustrating.

Anyway, this particular W. B. Yeats: Selected Poems[4] (by Gramercy Books) seems to be out in a variety of versions (and covers), but can be had for as little as a penny (in a "like new" copy of the hardcover), so it you are interested in catching up on Yeats' early work, it won't set you back much.

Notes:

1. http://btripp-books.livejournal.com/116273.html
2. http://www.open-books.org/
3-4. http://amzn.to/1mz7Fo4

Tuesday, August 23, 2011[1]

Humor, history, and (reasonably) current events ...

A week or so back I'd run up to the dollar store to pick up a bunch of stuff that we'd needed that I knew they had up there, after not having been there is a while. One of the "new things" I found were several shelf-loads of new books. As regular readers of this space know, in the many years that I've been "between jobs" I've learned to pinch pennies, and one of the best book deals out there are the ones that find their way to the dollar store, as even if the on-line new/used guys have something for 1¢, you still need to pay $3.99 shipping on it, where a book at the dollar store is, obviously, *a dollar*. While there were a number of books that looked "plausible", I really wasn't in a "book acquiring" mood (hey, it happens from time to time), but *was* in the mood for "something ~~completely~~ reasonably different" to inject into my reading, and a humor book seemed like a good bet for that.

This is how [Dave Barry's History of the Millennium (So Far)][2] not only found its way *into* my to-be-read pile, it moved right into the reading rotation in a day or so. Now, it's evident that this was not a particularly strongly considered purchase, so I came to the book with a bare minimum of data ... familiar with the author, reasonably interested in the subject, open to delving into the genre ... but not much else. So, of course, I was a bit surprised. It turns out that this was a clever way to re-package Barry's end-of-year columns, recapping the events of the year (in varying degrees of wacky re-telling). He starts the book off, however, with 33 pages on the *last* millennium ... compacting a thousand years of history (1,000ce to 1999ce) into a sixth of a just-over 200 page book. Needless to say, if "brevity is the soul of wit", this level of abbreviation allows for quite the witty recitation of history.

There appears to be another reason for this intro chapter, however. The book came out in 2007, and "the Millennium (So Far)" should have encompassed seven chapters, one each for 2000 through 2006, but the 2001 installment fell victim to the 9/11 national funk, as Barry would have been starting work on that year's edition a few weeks after the attacks, and he opted to take a pass rather that either being inappropriately humorous, or becoming untowardly serious. So, I'm guessing, the "Y1K" review was standing in for that dark year.

So, what we have here is a re-use of six of Dave Barry's end-of-the-year columns, wrapped up with an intro and put out as a book. This is not a *bad* thing, but it does imply that there are no great story arcs or narratives waiting in its pages. Each of the yearly chapters averages around 30 pages, and is divided up by monthly sections, meaning that each month gets about 2-3 pages of "news" reported. Most of this is "funny stuff inspired by the news" (with running gags each year of stories that just wouldn't die, like Greta VanSusteren reporting on every story "from Aruba"), but a few things were pulled straight from the news:

> *True item: In the War on Smoking, several states take legal steps to protect major tobacco companies from an anticipated huge damage award in a class action lawsuit. The states need the tobacco companies to say in business, because, thanks to the tobacco settlement, the states now make more money from the sale of cigarettes than the tobacco companies do. If this makes no sense to you, it's because you're a human, as opposed to a lawyer.*

This was another odd find at the dollar store because the book does appear to still be in print, selling at the on-line guys at *full cover* ($22.95), while like-new copies are in the used channel for a penny plus shipping ... go figure! If this sounds like a fun read to you, your best bet would be to check the dollar stores, but it's out there for cheap on-line as well.

Notes:

1. http://btripp-books.livejournal.com/116534.html
2. http://amzn.to/1RzYuk7

Sunday, August 28, 2011[1]

Next she'll say he had no Katanas ...

While I've not read Dan Brown's "DaVinci Code" books, I've read many books from which the inspiration for those was drawn, as well as others discussing them and the subsequent movies. While much of this genre is certainly "odd", Sangeet Duchane's <u>Beyond the Da Vinci Code: From the Rose Line to the Bloodline</u>[2] stands out as a "huh?" book.

I frankly don't recall how I ended up with this in my collection (yes, I know, that's odd in and of itself!), but I suspect that I got it via a B&N sale, either in the store or on-line, but it is *possible* that this might have come from the dollar store at some point, The provenance of this is an interesting question, as it's a large-format hard-cover book printed on heavy gloss paper with hundreds of color illustrations, a real "deluxe" edition with an original cover price of a very minimal $15.95 ... and you know I didn't pay that for it. What I wonder (and this almost gets into Dan Brown "conspiracy theory" zones) is who felt this book was worthy of this sort of presentation, and did it have a *prayer* of making any money at that price point?

To indulge further into the "conspiracy" realm, it's very hard to find any information about Sangeet Duchane herself, aside from a very brief author bio which says she was a lawyer who went back to school to get a Masters in Theology, and focused on "feminine spirituality". She has several books out, but very little other info floating around about her.

The elements of the "sacred feminine" that are in the "DaVinci Code" books are obviously the point of contact which seems to have been the genesis of this book, but the book is odd in that it's neither "rooting for" nor specifically aimed at debunking Brown's work. It's as though the author took the opportunity of the popularity of those books and movies to step into the fray with her own message.

Honestly, I wasn't expecting *as much* debunking of Brown as there is in here. I'm guessing there's about a 5-to-1 ratio of her saying that Brown is baseless on some point to those which are agreeing with him. She's evidently rather disdainful of Brown's research and presentation over-all, yet utilizes the subjects that he raises to take a look at the realities there, generally spun to a "feminine spirituality" perspective.

<u>Beyond the Da Vinci Code</u>[3] is in five parts: The Early Church, The Sacred Feminine, The Holy Grail, Leonardo Da Vinci, and Modern Times. In these she looks at assorted elements of myth, history, re-written history (the eradication of the feminine aspects in the Church, etc.), all the Baigent / Leigh / Lincoln (and related) material, and things that have developed over the centuries.

Again, the author, while on some level *sympathetic* with Brown's approach to "uncovering the misdeeds of the Church", spends much of the book in a "well, it really wasn't like that" mode, showing how some things in the DVC books are impossible, some are misinterpreted, some are purely invention, and some are, frankly, simply the results of poor to non-existent research. What I probably found most frustrating here was that she didn't generally come back with a *well-researched* slam at the Church ... most of these end up with some variant of "yes, these people are *horrible*, but not horrible in the way they're depicted by Brown".

As such, the book floats off in a grey area ... not supporting Brown, but being against the (documented) perversions of the Church, debunking much of what's in the DVC books, but not replacing it with her own broadsides ... and I suspect that this would be a fairly frustrating read for anybody coming to it "with a dog in the fight" (of course, I can't speak for the "feminine spirituality" camp, perhaps this reads just great to them!), or even just an interest in Brown's vision.

As a former publisher, I'm somewhat amazed at the *physical* nature of the book, the big format, the extremely high-quality "art book" paper, the massive amount of full color illustration, and, as noted, the very low cover price (this could easily have been priced 3-4 times what it was). Somebody wanted this to go out with a splash ... and get into a lot of hands.

Speaking of which ... if this sounds like something you'd like to check out ... it's available *new* in the big deluxe hardcover for **1¢** (plus, of course the $3.99 shipping) from the new/used guys on Amazon. Amazing. While being "frustrating", it's not a bad read, and it's an awesome looking book, so picking up a cheap copy might be something you'd want to consider!

Notes:

1. http://btripp-books.livejournal.com/116810.html

2-3. http://amzn.to/1mz6yEX

Monday, August 29, 2011[1]

What to do, what to do ...

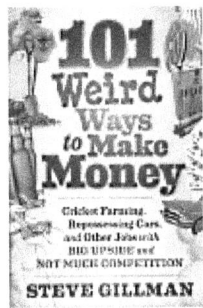

As you may recall, I noted a few reviews back that I'd gotten a box of recently released books from the good folks at Wiley, and Steve Gillman's 101 Weird Ways to Make Money: Cricket Farming, Repossessing Cars, and Other Jobs With Big Upside and Not Much Competition[2] was among those. I don't know what specifically made me bump this up to the top of the to-be-read pile, but I suspect that it might be some angst that I've been feeling with my own job situation ... as regular readers are probably aware, I'm about to be in my 28th month "between jobs", and, while I've had some situations which looked very promising for my being hired (and periods when I've had nearly full-time work doing freelance and consulting), I'm pretty much back to "square one" again, and I think on one level I was hoping that Gillman's book would prod me into some "out of the box" thinking.

There's a wonderful *bon mot* from the late Johnny Carson that I've found very useful to keep in mind over the years: *"It takes all types to fill the freeway!"*, and this certainly is the case when looking at this book, as its author has held *dozens* of jobs in widely divergent settings, which makes the premise here a bit more reality-based than it might be. I, on the other hand, have pretty much always been in some form of "communications" work, so making a jump into most of the things in 101 Weird Ways to Make Money[3] would likely be some sort of desperation move (much like when I attempted bartending after my publishing company failed).

Frankly, there aren't that many "weird" ways to make money here, but I'm sure that's a catchier title than something referring to "niche" jobs, which would likely be a more accurate descriptor. The 101 jobs discussed are spread out over 12 sections, in which they're thematically grouped. These are:

1. *Fun Ways to Make Money*
2. *Making Money Outdoors*
3. *Dirty and Ugly Jobs*
4. *Internet Opportunities*
5. *Green Jobs and Businesses*
6. *Home-Based Money Makers*
7. *Working with People*
8. *Working with Animals*
9. *Creative and Artistic Work*
10. *Buying and Selling Things*
11. *Cleaning Jobs and Businesses*
12. *Still More Unusual Ways to Make Money*

Each of these starts with an introductory piece with an interview with somebody involved in one of the jobs, and contains five to fifteen Chapters, each dealing with a particular type of job. Each job is given only 2 pages, so this hardly provides an in-depth look at any, but each short "chapter" is structured with a couple of paragraphs of description, a couple of paragraphs on "Money", a couple of paragraphs on "How To Get Started", and a "Resources" section with a list of suggested books and web sites.

Many of the "jobs" here are presented as "foot in the door" entrees to moving into small business ownership, with a lot of the information being on how much it would cost to get set up and trained in these. The "Money" section does give estimates on how much these would pay, but the general thrust is towards opening up one's own operation (after all, how many staff openings are there in Worm Grunting or Cricket Farming?). The author likely approaches the subject in this manner as, frankly, most of the jobs discussed don't pay very much "unless you're the boss" (and, in which case, one *can* make six figures with most of these).

That being said, the writing is engaging and informative, and the jobs *do* tend to be things that one might not have considered (Rodeo Clown, Mattress Recycler, Garbage Truck Washer, etc., etc., etc.) ... although I must admit, most of the things in the "Internet Opportunities" section I *have* looked into at one point or another.

101 Weird Ways to Make Money[4] is brand new (it just came out last month), so it should be available at the bigger "brick & mortar" book stores, but both of the on-line guys have it at around a 45% discount, so that's likely to be your best bet for picking it up. Again, while very few of the 101 things in here "struck my fancy", it's an interesting look at a lot of work possibilities!

Notes:

1. http://btripp-books.livejournal.com/117090.html

2-4. http://amzn.to/20Su6rg

Thursday, September 1, 2011[1]

Theravada training ...

Ah, the mysteries of the Newberry Library Book Fair[2] ... there are always strange inclusions that one wonders came from a private collector, now deceased, a library moving out old volumes, or what. As I've noted in previous reviews of books from that over the years, sometimes there are dedications, book plates, or assorted ephemera which can give you some idea of how that particular (old) book found its way to one of the many dozen tables across the ground floor of the Newberry, but this time I drew a blank.

Not only did I draw a blank, the current volume didn't even have an ISBN, or even particularly specific publication data (although it does have info on the printer and an address, of the author, to send donations if one was so inclined). According to the (unnamed) Translators' preface (from July of 1989) the author, Phra Ācariya Thoon Khippapañño, is an *"abbot of a forest monastery in northeastern Thailand"* who has written several books, Beyond the Stream of the World[3] being one of a series.

I bring this up because this slim volume isn't the typical "Buddhism book" out there, as the author is writing very much from a narrow context, and, while the book *is* targeted to a novice audience, it is coming out of the specific Theravada environment, so has notable differences (most notably in spellings here) from the more familiar Mahayana branches of India, Tibet (Vajrayana), and Japan (Zen). Much of this book is focused on having the student study the "right" materials and practices, which, obviously, relates to this focus. Here's a bit from one of the introductory sections:

> *The practice on mind development is a very delicate process. It involves all-round knowledge to avoid possible misunderstandings. It is not the case that all the realizations, which arise in the course of the practice, are true, because these realizations can arise from two different sources: Right View and Wrong View. The two lead to completely different ends. The knowledge gained from right views teaches the mind and raises it to a higher level of Dhamma practice in line with the Noble Path (Magga), which leads to the Final Goal (Nibbána), the cessation of all defilements and suffering. In contrast, knowledge from wrong views leads the mind in a wrong direction forever, and the chance of returning to the right line of Dhamma is very remote.*

While the book is quite short, it's also quite intense, and one gets the impression that this was developed our of work with young monks who needed to be "whipped into shape", and much of this stern hand finds its way onto the pages here. The book is in two sections, the main "discussion" comprising 22 topics, plus an appendix which presents a number of approaches to a walking and sitting meditation. I suppose it's a tribute to the author that this is a very dense, and at points difficult, read ... as a lot of books of its size would be far less challenging, and there is little here that does not demand to be chewed over with deliberate concentration!

In the "Concluding Remarks" section, the author writes:

> "A Dhamma student must use wisdom to find a deft way to eradicate harmful memories, suppositions and fabricated thoughts from the mind, using mindfulness to restrain the heart and wisdom to contemplate the negative side of sights, sounds, etc., at all times."

... which at that point is very cogent, clear, and comprehensible, not, what I would guess, would be most readers' reactions coming to this cold.

As such, I have to give this credit for being a very effective introductory book to the author's school of Buddhist thought ... he presents a fairly complete over-view of the religion, addresses many points which are essential to the practitioner, and sets up the basic structure for the student to follow, then adds on practical instruction in key meditations.

Again, Beyond the Stream of the World[4] is not an "easy read" but it's a "quality read" for a background in Theravada. It appears that these are intended for free distribution, and while a couple of copies "are out there" from the usual suspects, you might look closer to the source for a copy. In fact, I found a couple of groups operating out of Malaysia (HERE[5] and HERE[6]) which offer to send out free books (and they have close to a hundred titles each), just requesting that you send them the equivalent of the postage once you've received the books. However, I've also discovered that the text of the book is also available on-line at the DharmaWeb[7] site ... which, needless to say, would be your most cost-effective way to go if you don't need to have the dead-tree version in hand!

Notes:
1. http://btripp-books.livejournal.com/117303.html
2. http://go.newberry.org/bookfair
3-4. http://amzn.to/1TOkkP2
5. http://reocities.com/wave_books/freebooks.htm
6. http://www.dhammatalks.net/Free_Dhamma_Books.htm
7. http://www.dharmaweb.org/index.php/Beyond_The_Stream_Of_The_World_By_Phra_Acariya_Thoon_Khippapanno

Sunday, September 11, 2011[1]

Hard to believe ...

This was one of those "because it's there" pick-ups that I didn't put much planning or intent into, but none the less ended up worthwhile. I'd been having a planning meeting regarding an upcoming project over at my usual B&N Cafe, and they had a couple of tables of books and stuff at 75% off I dug through there and found a couple of things that "looked interesting" (unfortunately, the other was something that I had in hardcover, and I didn't recognize it in a much-redesigned paperback edition).

This is to say that I did not set out to add to my reading about the Mormon church, but figured it wouldn't hurt to have something else in the library. The Pearl of Great Price[2] is by Joseph Smith, the founder of the Church of Jesus Christ of Latter Day Saints, and is sort of the "backstory" about how he founded it. According to the quite informative introductory essay, this had been edited quite a bit over the years, but as it presently stands, it's about three-quarters "revelatory texts" (similar to what's in the Book of Mormon) with the rest being various pieces written by Smith.

The two "revealed" texts are "The Book of Moses" and "The Book of Abraham", the former being "revealed" to him in 1830, and the latter being "translated" by him from copies made of some Egyptian papyrus. They are quite different, no doubt due to the variation of the "revelation".

The "Book of Moses" begins with Moses talking to God "face-to-face" and being tested by Satan, and passing the test and sort of getting as a reward a whole walk-through of what had happened from "let there be light" on up to these conversations (and beyond). There is a whole lot of begetting and forming of peoples, and moving around, and falling away from God, and getting in league with Satan, much along the lines of what is in the Bible. However, it is interesting how Satan is credited with "a secret" which those that *do* fall in league with him use to succeed:

> 49. For Lamech having entered into a covenant with Satan, after the manner of Cain, wherein he became Master Mahan, mater of the great secret which was administered unto Cain by Satan; and Irad, the son of Enoch, having known their secret, began to reveal it unto the sons of Adam;
>
> 50. Wherefore Lamech, being angry, slew him, no like unto Cain his brother Abel, for the sake of getting gain, but he slew him for that oath's sake.
>
> 51. For, from the days of Cain, there was a secret combination, and their works were in the dark, and they knew every man his brother.

Needless to say, this is a fascinating concept! One of the things that I found irritating here is that the whole narrative is set up with repeated references to Jesus, sort of like re-telling the Old Testament with Christian assumptions built in. I suppose that some Christians do this anyway, but it's somewhat jarring to have repeated "but of course it works out this way" anachronistic references in the pre-Mosaic narrative!

The "Book of Abraham" is supposedly a translation Smith made of some papyrus texts that came into his possession in 1835. Now, it is *possible* to have a translation of Ancient Egyptian writings by that date, as the first bits of the language were coming to light in the 1820s, but the odds that Smith did anything more than "riff" on his impressions of what was in them (reminding me of a friend with no computer training who claimed he could "read" binary machine code!) is pretty slim. There are three reproductions (of ink brush copies made of the "conveniently" lost originals) here and in each case *anybody* (today) who had studied Ancient Egypt would know that Smith was making some *whoppers* in his "translation" (a glaring example is saying that the scene with a Goddess {either Hathor or Isis} standing behind the enthroned Osiris with Maat facing him is presented as the Pharaoh standing behind *Abraham* with a prince facing him ... I found more details on this here: http://www.mormonthink.com/book-of-abraham-issues.htm[3]). Since all things Egyptian were "hot" at the time, it's quite likely that this was Smith just going for some "popular" ancient heritage.

In the remaining parts of the book, Smith outlines his history, with many sections of nearly cynical views of the "unusual excitement on the subject of religion", where sect vied against sect, preacher against preacher, and congregation against congregation. I had intended to copy some of that out here, but it would have run to at least a half a page before it became coherent, so I've opted not to.

As with so much in "revealed" religions, you either take the author's word that stuff happened the way he says (angels coming down out of the sky to tell him what to write or do), or you don't. Needless to say, most of this is pretty hard to accept as "real". However, there are bits and pieces here which are just so *weird* that one wonders *why* these elements would pass a cursory edit of the material ... most notably an encounter with an "angel" who manifested in his room, enveloped in bright light, and gave him various revelations and instructions, then ascending into the heavens (through the ceiling, I take it), only to momentarily to re-appear, *"and again related the very same things which he had done at his first visit, without the least variation"*, and then *again* a third time, as though the whole thing were some holographic message stuck on "replay"!

Frankly, the very bizarreness of this account almost supports its veracity, if suggesting to the modern mind something other than a metaphysical source. Of course, is the back-story of the Mormon faith any stranger than what most other religions ask people to believe? The pastiche of middle eastern myth that supports (standard) Christianity is no more convincing that Zenu and volcanoes, or every "convenient" "revelation" that supports other faiths (I've always liked Napoleon's quip that "God fights on the side with the best artillery."). One has to give props, however, to a Church that includes the following in their "Articles of Faith":

> 11. We claim the privilege of worshiping Almighty God according to the dictates of our own conscience, and allow all men the same privilege, let them worship how, where, or what they may.

Heck, that could be an out-take from Liber Al (and maybe Crowley cribbed from Joseph Smith there)!

Anyway, The Pearl of Great Price[4] is "a classic" (this edition is from "The Barnes & Nobel Library of Essential Reading") and it's still available from BN.com (and the Amazon new/used guys) ... however, because of its age it seems to be out of copyright, and you can get it free on-line (courtesy the Mormons) here: http://lds.org/scriptures/pgp?lang=eng[5] ... which, obviously would be your best bet price-wise.

Notes:

1. http://btripp-books.livejournal.com/117539.html
2. http://amzn.to/1TOiSMK
3. http://www.mormonthink.com/book-of-abraham-issues.htm
4. http://amzn.to/1TOiSMK
5. http://lds.org/scriptures/pgp?lang=eng

Wednesday, September 14, 2011[1]

A peek behind the curtains ...

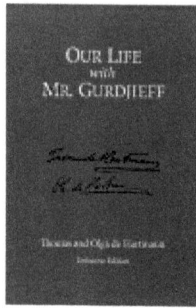

As regular readers of these reviews know, I primarily read non-fiction, so it is a rare case (much of what I read tends to be "on the dry side") when I hit a book that I can barely put down. Our Life with Mr. Gurdjieff[2] by Thomas & Olga de Hartmann was, delightfully, one of these. This is a very interesting book, as it is a relatively recent combination of Thomas de Hartmann's memoirs (which stopped mid-sentence upon his death in 1956), which had been widely published previously, with the unpublished memoirs of his widow, Olga, who continued in the Gurdjieff work until her death in 1979.

The editorial team here (two generations of Thomas Daleys) were given open access to Mrs. de Hartmann's archives and went back to the original manuscripts to make a fresh translation from Russian to English. They then took the two, Thomas' much longer text, and the notes that Olga had written, and shuffled them together in proper chronology, putting her copy in italics interspersed with his narrative. As noted above, Thomas' material ceased rather abruptly, and Olga had added a ten-page or so "conclusion" which brought the story to a close, and the editors have added to this a "Chronology" to make it easier to follow the activities of the book.

If you are not familiar with the teachings of G.I. Gurdjieff, you are missing one of the seminal sources of much of recent "western metaphysics", expanding largely through his students P.D. Ouspensky and J.G. Bennett and their students and associates. If I were to recommend starting points, I'd say to read Gurdjieff's *Meetings With Remarkable Men* and Ouspensky's *In Search of the Miraculous*, both of which are fascinating. Gurdjieff claimed to have been part of a "working group" of "seekers" who combed the world seeking out authentic ancient knowledge, the results of which search he had synthesized into his system. Here's a particularly direct reference to this from the book:

> *In esoteric schools there were men of high attainment who studied the nature of a man as a whole. Their pupils were people who wished to develop their being. They spoke sincerely and openly about their inner search, how to achieve their aim, how to approach it, and of their characteristics that stood in the way. To go to such real confession one had to make a major decision: to see one's real defects and to speak about them. Mr. Gurdjieff told us that this was absolutely essential – especially for one to see his chief feature, the one around which (as around an axis) turn all his stupid, comical, secondary weaknesses.*

However, this is jumping ahead a bit, as the book is more about the de Hartmann's *relationship* and *activities* with Gurdjieff than about "the work" particularly.

The book starts in the middle of WWI, in 1915, beginning in St. Petersburg with Russian minor noble de Hartmann entering the military. He was already a composer and musician of note, and through this and his connections he is transferred to the Guard, and generally spared the worse parts of the War. He and Olga had been seeking out "teachers" and at one point he is introduced (in circumstances most untoward for a Guards officer) to Gurdjieff, and the connection sticks, and he and Olga decide to follow Gurdjieff no matter what.

Of course, the war is quickly followed by the revolution, and for most of the book the de Hartmanns and other students are trekking across Russia attempting to stay out of the way of the conflict (and especially the Bolsheviks, who would have shot him on sight). Again, this is not so much a book about "the work" but of their "Life with Mr. Gurdjieff", and it's certainly a different window onto this remarkable situation than many of the other books out there. The action follows them to southern Russia, the Crimea, Constantinople, Berlin, and eventually to Paris, and the famed Institute in the suburbs thereof, and finally to America.

This has elements of a biography, a travelogue, a metaphysical memoir, and an adventure story. There is very little "uneventful" material here ... probably because so much of Gurdjieff's "work" involved setting up challenging situations for his students to work through. De Hartmann is constantly having to battle dual responsibilities of being a student, *and* Gurdjieff's main musical interpreter. There is a significant body of material that was developed for various "exhibitions" produced by Gurdjieff, in Paris, New York, and elsewhere, which is still available. I've not heard much of this, but it's been on my list to get, given the right situation.

Now, obviously, I came to this book with a lot of "background" and being familiar with the characters (interestingly, the grandfather of one of my high-school friends figures in here, as he had been the personal physician to the Tsar and one of his houses features in the story), and the philosophical underpinnings, my impression of the tale is different from that of one who had little or no knowledge of "all things Gurdjieff". While *I* immensely enjoyed reading this, I wonder if it would be as engaging to one "coming to it cold", and, as such, I need to offer the caveat that this is a *delightful* book about some of Gurdjieff's followers' experiences with him, but it might end up being confusing if this is one's first exposure the genre. On the other hand, this is not a "dense" book on "the work" and so should be more accessible than some that jump right into the metaphysical depths.

Our Life with Mr. Gurdjieff[3] is available for a very reasonable price (at about twelve bucks) from the on-line guys, and the Morning Light Press softcover edition is new this year, so the brick-and-mortar vendors that carry philosophical and metaphysical titles might well have copies too. However, do make sure you're getting the new edition, as earlier versions don't have Mrs. de Hartmann's contributions and are in a possibly less-focused translation. I liked it a lot, and (with the books recommended above), I'd think it's a good read for anybody!

Notes:

1. http://btripp-books.livejournal.com/117938.html

2-3. http://amzn.to/1TOhdH2

Saturday, October 22, 2011[1]

Picture this ...

From time to time I get books from publishers that I wonder what I'm going to do with ... and when I got a package from Random House's Crown division's Amphoto Books imprint, I was initially wondering why. However, once I made my way through Going Pro: How to Make the Leap from Aspiring to Professional Photographer[2] by Scott Bourne & Skip Cohen, I figured out that their promo department had done a pretty good job of targeting this, at least in terms of my The Job Stalker[3] blog over on the Tribune's "Chicago Now" site.

Although I have, over the years, had a varying level of enthusiasm for photography, I've never given it much thought as a *career*, and this led me to wonder what I'd be able to get out of a book so obviously targeted to those who *were* thinking along those lines. After all, the *specifics* here address a level of photography that I'd never been involved in, although I'm assuming that these are things familiar to more serious photographers (for instance, I've never made a photographic print since *summer camp* back in grade school!). So on the fine-level, this is a book that's way over the heads of me, and most other casual photographers, or those even less involved with cameras than that. However, if one pulls back the focus, the *broad strokes* here are certainly applicable to most anybody who had considered taking an avocation and turning it into their main vocation.

The book begins with "Define Your Niche", where it's noted *"You will be miles ahead if you focus ... on that which you are most passionate about and which you are most intimate with – that which you love and know the most about."* ... this is clearly advice that would apply to any effort to build a career out of activities you're immersed in. This section then goes into descriptions of various photographic categories, with info on each ... again, while the details may not be for the general reader, the message there is certainly applicable across a wide range of interests and activities.

The book moves on with "Be the Best Photographer You Can Be", where the importance of honing one's craft is presented, to "Test the Water and Show Your Work", which is, perhaps, more to the photographic field than others, to "Marketing", "Social Media Marketing for Photographers", "Use Twitter to Grow Your Photo Business", "Blogging: Your Online Presence", "The World of Search", "Old-Fashioned Networking", "Expand Your Business", and "Outsourcing". Needless to say, these last eight chapters have material which can be brought to bear in any field. Again, the details are about how to develop one's *photographic* business, but the advice and most of the resources could be well taken in the move from a dedicated hobbyist to a professional in assorted fields.

Obviously, Going Pro[4] is addressed to a very narrow population, but if you have an interest in photography (it is, as one would expect, lushly filled with examples of professional work, and the entire book is printed on high-quality paper), you may find this of interest. Also, as noted, this is a book that anybody who might be considering making "what they love to do" into "what they do" would find a lot of useful material.

This only "officially" came out this week, so it should be available in your local brick-and-mortar stores, but the big on-line guys currently have it at a substantial discount. Scott Borune "is known as the #1 photographer on Twitter" (whatever that means), and I'm assuming that this, and the activities of Skip Cohen (publishing, conferences, schools), leads to a particular "spin" here ... but the main take-away I had here was that this had use beyond the bounds of photography ... so it might be something that you'd find of interest.

Notes:

1. http://btripp-books.livejournal.com/118245.html
2. http://amzn.to/1OcKR7i
3. http://jobstalker.info/
4. http://amzn.to/1OcKR7i

Sunday, October 23, 2011[1]

A time to rend, a time to sew

I've had this one sitting around for a while ... it came in via one of those BN.com on-line sales where the prices are low and the descriptions are brief, and I end up with more than a few "pig in a poke" acquisitions. Now, one of my four majors in college (OK, I only fully *completed* two) was Religion, and I still get the itch to read stuff that's more "academic" than my usual list, and this seemed to fit the bill a few weeks back. Needless to say, Rhetoric and Kairos: Essays in History, Theory, and Praxis[2], edited by Phillip Sipiora & James S. Baumlin, is not exactly "light reading", but I found the concept of "Kairos" fascinating, and wondered why it hadn't "gotten into my head" back in college.

To "cut to the chase", Kairos is one of the concepts of time developed by the ancient Greeks, along with Chronos and Aion ... Chronos being the "flowing" sequential time of daily experience, what the clock tracks, Aion being "eternal" time, or what appears to me to be the fourth axis of a 4-dimensional space, with Kairos being "the right time", or "opportunity" (based on the Latin translation of Kairos). Kairos then dovetails with propriety and efficiency ... the word itself appears to have come from ancient archery as being the moment when an arrow could pass through interspersing obstacles to find its target (I can't help to think of a football pass that splits tight double coverage to end up in the arms of the receiver). The *concept* is fairly common, but not so much in the terminology. The English translation of the Bible frequently places Kairos in terms of "a time to", much like in Ecclesiastes 3:1 (or The Byrds' *Turn! Turn! Turn!*) "To every thing there is a season".

However, rather than being a book *about* Kairos, what the editors have produced is a series of academic papers that deal with Kairos in a variety of contexts, largely assembled in a chronological order. As is often the case with collections of disparate materials like this, the tone and structure of each paper differs, making the reading experience uneven (not that one would pick up Rhetoric and Kairos[3] for light "enjoyment" reading anyway). The first seven pieces here discuss the concept of Kairos, and how it functioned within the context of Ancient Greece, and in the writings of several famed philosophers. As one would expect from the title, much of the focus here is on the *rhetorical* applications in Athens and elsewhere.

The book then moves into looks at Kairos in the New Testament, in Roman writings, in the Renaissance, in Shakespeare's *Hamlet*, in the writings of Ralph Waldo Emerson, in the arts, in "composition classes", and closes with a proposition for an "ethics of Kairos".

Being that I got this via a clearance sale, I was surprised to find that it is still available via the on-line guys, which leads me to think that this is likely a college text book. It is also listed with them without any discount *and* there are no "cheap" copies in the used channels (although there are some there at less than half of cover). Of course, I doubt anybody reading this is *aching* to pick up a copy (it is both academic and a bit obscure), but if it sounds like something you'd find of interest, it is at least something you can order.

Notes:

1. http://btripp-books.livejournal.com/118375.html

2-3. http://amzn.to/1mOn30F

Monday, October 24, 2011[1]

This is a fun book ...

As regular readers of this space will no doubt recognize, it is (due to my now long-term unemployment) a rare thing for me to actually buy a book for cover price (or even Amazon's discounted price), so when I do so, as is the case here, it says something about my attraction to a particular title. I have been a fan of Penn & Teller for a very long time ... I used to use dial-up (at 300 baud) on long-distance lines to New York back in the 80's to get into their "Mofo Ex Machina" BBS, and was always looking forward to Penn's columns in PC-Computing magazine back in the early 90's, and have followed Penn in his various projects on Twitter, so it was unsurprising that I was very much looking forward to Penn Jillette's God, No!: Signs You May Already Be an Atheist and Other Magical Tales[2] when it came out this Fall.

Penn, of course, is a noted Libertarian and Atheist, and I certainly share a lot of viewpoints with him (although he'd belittle my agnosticism, as he clearly does in here), and I was perfectly willing to be "the choir" to which he was preaching in this, but I was surprised to see how uneven the book was. Nominally, the book is structured to parallel the "Ten Commandments", with a section for each containing one to four essays, more-or-less relating to the subject of each commandment. Unfortunately, the "more-or-less" frequently veers into the "less" side of things with stories that have very little to do with Atheism, and more with generally painting Penn as a goof (the much-promo'd "hairdryer" piece being prime among these) with "TMI" for anyone.

Of course, when Penn's good, he's *very* good ... and here are a few choice bits:

> It's not fair to blame all the Muslims for the horrible acts of a few people. That's wrong. You cannot blame all those people. And we shouldn't blame a particular faith for the horrible acts of a few people. At least we shouldn't blame just Islam. We should blame all faiths. We should blame faith in general. But Bush and Obama couldn't do that. No religious person can do that. Being religious means being okay with believing in things without evidence. That's the most important part of any faith. Catholics say that questioning is bad; Jews say questioning is good; but they all say that faith is a-okay. They have to. The deal religious folks make with each other is: we'll argue about the specifics of our separate bugnutty crazy, but the general idea of being bugnutty crazy is good. Once you've condoned faith in general, you've condoned any crazy shit done because of faith.

I had intended to put in a different paragraph here, but it's been rendered a meme out on the web (see HERE[3]) and would be redundant for me to type it up for this review, however, a supporting paragraph says:

> People try to argue that government isn't really force. You believe that? Try not paying your taxes (This is only a thought experiment – suggesting someone not pay their taxes is probably a federal offense, and I'm a nut, but I'm not crazy.) When they come to get you for not paying your taxes, try not going to court. Guns will be drawn. Government is force – literally, not figuratively.

And then there's this:

> Just about everyone who writes and produces comedy on TV is a {f'n} lefty and is pushing the agenda of gay rights and liberal causes, and my liberal friends – even though they're against the {f'n} corporations running TV – are thrilled with those writers, but when the {f'n} psycho right wing says the TV writers are doing just what they're doing, my liberal friends scoff. I think that's why my lefty friends are so comfortable calling the Tea Party people racist, even though the Tea Party doesn't say they themselves are racist. My lefty friends just assume that everyone lies about their real agenda.

This is the sort of stuff I was waiting to read, and not the bits about … well, you really do have to go get the details of "the blowdryer story" for yourself.

Now, let me be perfectly clear … this is an *awesome* book … it's a good 70% great stuff, but the off-topic bits stand out like a sore (oh, man, I'm missing a easy joke here) thumb, and make me wonder just how much "editorial guidance" Penn had on God, No![4]. Again, not that the "off" bits here weren't amusing in their own right, I just wish he'd "kept on target" here, and saved those other bits for the start of a new book ("Penn's TMI" would be a nice title, no?).

This has been out for a few months, and must be doing very well (the used guys have copies out, but only for a buck or so less than the on-line discount price), so I'm sure you'd be able to find a copy pretty much anywhere that carries new books, but both Amazon and B&N have it for 41% off of cover, which makes it a pretty sweet deal. Again, I loved the book, just not as much as I had hoped to … I'd recommend it to anybody who appreciates Libertarianism or the Atheist side ("not collecting stamps") of the religious spectrum, and (with my Discordian leanings) to all and sundry (especially those who are fond of "F-bombs" in print). I do feel, however, that this is another example of a volume where a firmer editorial hand would have made a very good book a classic.

Notes:

1. http://btripp-books.livejournal.com/118636.html
2. http://amzn.to/1mOkTyc
3. http://goo.gl/UACVBW
4. http://amzn.to/1mOkTyc

Counting on it ...

This book found its way into my hands via the LibraryThing.com "Early Reviewers" program, having been matched with my on-line library[2] by the LTER "almighty algorithm" in the July batch. Unfortunately, the book did not *arrive* until early October, sort of missing the "early" in "Early Reviewers" for a book that came out the first week of July! Oh, well, I had plenty of other things to read.

Anyway, I was somewhat surprised to have been matched up with Keith Devlin's The Man of Numbers: Fibonacci's Arithmetic Revolution[3], not having a lot of *mathematical* books in my collection, although, I suppose, quite a number of biographical books on figures in science and philosophy. This is very much more a look at *the man* (and a piecing together of his history), rather than the mathematics, per se, so I guess that makes sense.

Leonardo Pisano, filius Bonacci, was from Pisa (of the famed leaning tower), and from the Bonacci family, an attribute which eventually became condensed to "Fibonacci" over time. It appears that his father was a Customs official there, and had, in this role, much contact with the merchant classes, and the business communications of the day. At one point (around 1180-85 CE), Leonardo's father was posted to a North African city, Bugia (presently in Algeria), and, once established there, he sent for his teenage son to join him.

One of the points the author makes early on is how numbers and counting are so intrinsically intertwined with our modern existence that it hard to imagine a world where dealing with numbers was something of a specialty, the tools of certain trades. In the world that Leonardo Pisano grew up in, every major trade center was likely to have its own sets of weights, measures, and currency, and the calculations were done with either complex finger computations (leading to the term "digit" surviving as a number notation) or worked out on an abacus ... neither of which lent themselves to preserving the details of the math. Also, in the European world, any *written* numbers were expressed in Roman numerals, which, due to their structure, were not very useful for anything other than addition and subtraction.

In Bugia, young Leonardo was exposed to the Islamic system of numbers, which had absorbed influences from India, including the concept of the place-keeping "0", and the three-place separations that we still use today (ie. 1,000,000). While this was not *unknown* in Europe (having come across with the Islamic invaders into Spain, etc. some centuries before), Leonardo saw the utility of this in the context of trade.

Frankly, he almost was forgotten to history, but his name survived in later math books that referred back to his publications. A great deal of The Man of Numbers[4] is tracking down the historical threads which lead back to Fibonacci and what survives of his books, and looking at the nature of these books from what remains. His main product, *Liber Abbaci* or "Book of Calculation" was a book of how to do calculations, and examples of these, and problems to be solved, a familiar format for math books ever since. However, the problems in his book were all "word problems", as modern "symbolic" notation hadn't been developed, so what we'd write as $x^2=40x-4x^2$ would be a whole paragraph of descriptive text.

The book tries to piece together the fragmented bits of Leonardo's biography and work, and fit these into the cultural milieu of his time, and the years following. It is fascinating that a figure like Leonardo, who is so well known for the mathematical entities that have come down from "Fibonacci", has been so little known in terms of his biography and bibliography. This reads something like a mystery, trying to prise this information out of surviving material (much of which sits untranslated in late medieval sources in various Italian cities) to get a clear look of the man and his work.

Obviously, this being out only a few months, The Man of Numbers[5] should be available in the more comprehensive brick-and-mortar book vendors. Of course, the on-line guys have it, with both of the big boys currently offering it at a 43% discount (with used copies coming in at right about the same price point so far). This was certainly an fascinating read, and anyone interested in math, the medieval world, or a story about researching obscure topics, should find this quite enjoyable.

Notes:

1. http://btripp-books.livejournal.com/118859.html

3. http://btripp-books.com/

3-5. http://amzn.to/1mOjuri

Wednesday, October 26, 2011[1]

Like a cyclone ranger ...

This was an acquisition from this Summer's Newberry Library Book Fair ... sometimes referred to as *"I buy dead people's books."* ... and, while this did not have any tell-tale information as to its previous owner, its vintage (pre-ISBN 1969) leads one to assume that whoever had done the minimal highlighting in this had expired. As I've mentioned previously, my habit for the NLBF is to show up on "Half-Price Sunday"; while this does make the books cheaper, it also means that there have been several days of the selection being picked over. While this is not a "happy thing" per se, it does put a rather significant limiter on my actual purchases. I was likely drawn to H. Byron Earhart's Japanese Religion, Unity and Diversity[2] due to it being in the Dickenson "The Religious Life of Man" series, and in a similar edition to those that I'd read in college.

The appeal here, of course, was "filling a gap" in my knowledge, having that Pokemon-esqe desire to "collect 'em all" when it comes to material in my varied areas of study ... in which Japanese religion was significantly under-represented. Frankly, this book provides a very handy encapsulation of Japanese *history*, as, obviously, the development of the intertwined religious manifestations occurs within the context of the culture, so this essentially is a 2-for-1 reading, providing data on both the history and religion.

The book starts with a general overview, and then jumps way back to the Neolithic era, which is when the first human traces appear in Japan, expressed in a hunting/gathering/fishing lifestyle, with evidence of burial rituals, and indications of typical fertility/fetishtic art. As Japanese culture evolved, so did these "native" religious elements, with one stream evolving into what was to be Shinto, with the shamanistic "Kami" spirits developing into a pantheon of deities such as the goddess Amaterasu, from whom the Imperial lineage is held to descend.

Japan, while somewhat isolated, still had a good deal of contact with its neighbors, and, in the sixth century CE, Buddhism came to it via Korea. As identified as Buddhism is (especially in the form of Zen) with Japanese culture, it's hard to think of it as a "foreign religion", but that was what it was at the time. Various schools established themselves in Japan, and there is a long history of their competition and vacillations of influence. A century or so later, Confucianism (along with Taoist trappings) also made its way over from China, and set up the main elements that were to be in play for the next centuries.

There is a lot of details on which sects were in control, in company with which political elements, from period to period, but there's no convenient way for me to work that in here. Of course, at one point Christianity got a toe-hold in Japan, creating another axis for political influence, but this largely stopped in the years following the 1614 edict banning Christianity, expelling the missionaries, and eventually leading to bloody purges.

Now, given as my copy of [Japanese Religion, Unity and Diversity](#)[3] is the 1969 edition, this specific volume is likely to be difficult to find ... however the on-line guys have copies of a later (1982) version for as little as one cent (plus shipping) for a "very good" copy. I rather enjoyed reading this, as it's fascinating info, stuff I hadn't known about (in detail) before, and reasonably engagingly written (for a college text). If you have an interest in how Buddhism, Shinto, Confucianism, Taoism, Zen and other offshoots developed in the Japanese cultural context, you might want to see about getting a copy from the Amazon used guys.

Notes:

1. http://btripp-books.livejournal.com/119207.html

2-3. http://amzn.to/1TO8ggJ

Tuesday, November 1, 2011[1]

Unlocking Secrets ...

As I read more in this genre, it becomes evident that the "alternative spirituality" that was so prevalent (in the Media, at least) in the 60's and 70's failed to set any significant roots, but *did* manage to alienate large portions of the population who either clung to their old religious myths, or held that if these things could not be *scientifically* proven, they didn't exist. It is so *odd* to be reading a widely-read book from 1945 which includes *telepathy* as a key element of processes that were evidently considered part of the daily habits of the captains of industry of the first half of the 20th Century, but there it is, and from the standpoint of 2011, it seems quite strange. Of course, over the past several years, on the heels of The Secret[2], and many books and self-help gurus mining the same vein, these "law of attraction" philosophies have gained new life, and this is one of the "sources" of this new movement.

Napoleon Hill's The Master Key to Riches[3] is (I believe) less well known than his *Think* and *Grow Rich*, but certainly follows a similar script. This book is set up as being the record of a presentation made to *"the largest audience ever assembled in the history of mankind"* by the masked *"richest man in the world"* ... needless to say, I'm assuming (lacking any trace of news coverage of such an event) this is purely a fictionalized setting for the story. The material here, like other of Hill's writings, points back to Andrew Carnegie as a source, along with Edison, Ford, and numerous others.

While reading The Master Key to Riches[4], I found echoes of other systems, either in the way they were presented (there is a slightly Gurdjieffian tone to bits of this), or in what they were implying ("the law of Cosmic Habitforce" here appears to have a number of parallels with certain aspects of Neuro-Linguistic Psychology), which lends a certain level of "maybe something's going on here" for what's being outlined. The main system of this is set out in a series of 17 "principles", and (to cut to the chase, as it were), I'll just set out:

 (a) The Habit of Going the Extra Mile
 (b) Definiteness of Purpose
 (c) The Master Mind
 (d) Applied Faith
 (e) Pleasing Personality
 (f) Habit of Learning from Defeat
 (g) Creative Vision
 (h) Personal Initiative
 (i) Accurate Thinking

(j) Self-Discipline
(k) Concentration of Endeavor
(l) Co-Operation
(m) Enthusasm
(n) The Habit of Health
(o) Budgeting Time and Money
(p) The Golden Rule *Applied*
(q) Cosmic Habitforce

Needless to say, I'm not going to take the space to try to provide much detail for these here. Most of these are fairly self-evident from their names, but others have quite a specific meaning, and are set out in further sub-lists. These have various levels of clarity (for me at least), from the muddle of the "Applied Faith" stuff to the almost sci-fi elements in the "Master Mind" section:

> "Every human brain is both a broadcasting station and a receiving station for the expression of the vibrations of thought, and the simulating effect of the Master Mind principle stimulates action of thought, through what is commonly known as telepathy, operating through the sixth sense."

I also found it interesting how much of the book reflects a "pre-progressive" view of America ... as a nation that through self-reliance, self-disciple, and personal initiative became great. It's a bitter reflection of how much of that spirit has been ground down by decade after decade of "progressive" intrusions by the government ... I doubt that Napoleon Hill would recognize the "nanny state" America that we have today, and I wonder how much of the system presented here could realistically be implemented in the over-regulated (and "entitled") morass of our current culture.

Again, my reaction to reading The Master Key to Riches[5] was very much like reading a text from a quite different world ... and I wonder how much a person can achieve with this system in the world we live in. Obviously, the elements here would be *quite helpful* to build up one's successes, but there's been nearly a century of advances by forces which are intrinsically inimical to individual advancement, and one thing that Hill didn't have to fight against when writing this was the tyranny of the herd.

Oh ... you want to know what "The Master Key" is? Well, "the speaker" doesn't so much put it up in PowerPoint slide, but, in the last few pages it gets around to saying that it's "The Power of Thought", obtained through *self-discipline* ... the elements of this are jumbled up sufficiently there that I didn't have a clear quote to stick in here, but there it is.

Many of the "source" books for the modern iteration of this genre are out there in the public domain, however, this, dating from mid-century, appears to not have made it into the free on-line versions as yet ... however, the *cover price* of the Dover edition that I picked up is under seven bucks, so it's not going to set you back too much to pick up a copy if this sounds like something you'd like to look into. As noted, this did not read to me like a "crystal clear" plan for personal achievement after 65 years of collectivist dismantling of the American dream since its publication, but there are some valuable structures here (it's *full* of lists and sub-lists of things to work on) which may well be useful despite the current situation.

Notes:

1. http://btripp-books.livejournal.com/119374.html

2. http://btripp-books.livejournal.com/33791.html

3-5. http://amzn.to/1JDUg8U

Friday, November 4, 2011[1]

An intense and hopeless despair ...

This was another of those books that I somehow missed on the way to my English major. Fortunately, it exists in a Dover Thrift Edition, so got added on to a sub-$25 Amazon order to get into free shipping land ... sort of a Law of Unintended Consequences thing for filling holes in my education! Of course, I *thought* that I knew what Joseph Conrad's Heart of Darkness[2] was about from having seen Apocalypse Now[3], which is largely based on this novella (although if you read the Wikipedia entry on the movie, there are several other literary sources), but I kept waiting for that familiarity to kick in, and it only rarely did.

And, as regular readers of this space know, it's a rare thing for me to be reading any fiction, so I'm a bit lost on what to say about this. My main takeaway was *"gee, that wasn't like the movie!"*, which being useful information to somebody else who was familiar with the Viet Nam version of the story, it would be met with a rather resounding *"DUH!"* for those who were coming to it expecting a tale from "deepest, darkest Africa".

The story is bracketed by small sections which take place on a ship in the Thames, with a handful of sailors sitting about and trading stories. One of whom, Marlow (who I take it to be a recurring character in Conrad's stories, something of a fictionalized version of himself), launches into telling a tale detailing his experiences from his youth leading him into a commercial posting that led him deep into the Congo. The main thrust of the story is his going upriver to secure the delivery of some ivory, requiring the renovation of a river boat, and overcoming assorted difficulties. Unlike in the movie, the protagonist is not on a mission to kill Kurtz (here a Mr., not a Col.), or even to specifically contact him, but Kurtz is a figure that many suggest is a remarkable man (*"Sends in as much ivory as all the others put together"*), and that their paths are likely to cross.

The writing is lush, which is probably why this has become such a classic ... how many writers do you know who could put together a passage like this:

> *The great wall of vegetation, an exuberant and entangled mass of trunks, branches, leaves, boughs, festoons, motionless in the moonlight, was like a rioting invasion of soundless life, a rolling wave of plants, piled up, crested, ready to topple over the creek, to sweep every little man of us out of his little existence. And it moved not.*

Of course, the downside of something this rich with description often loses a bit clarity of the narrative. Indeed, reading this has a certain dream-like aspect to it.

I understand that readers of fiction get very upset when reviewers put in "spoilers" … so, if you are unfamiliar with the story (either via the book or the movie), you may want to skip to the end at this point!

Perhaps the most recognizable parallel between the book and the movie is the death of Kurtz. Of course, the particulars of the two are quite different, but the key line survives:

> "Anything approaching the change that came over his features I have never seen before, and hope to never see again. Oh, I wasn't touched. I was fascinated. It was as though a veil had been rent. I saw on that ivory face the expression of somber pride, of ruthless power, of craven terror – of an intense and hopeless despair. Did he live his life again in every detail of desire, temptation, and surrender during that supreme moment of complete knowledge? He cried in a whisper at some image, at some vision – he cried out twice, a cry that was no more than a breath: 'The horror! The horror!'"

I have a hard time not seeing Marlon Brando, shaved head oozing feverish sweat, mumbling those words, crossed ever so slightly with *The Rugrats* (of all things) ironic take on it.

As I noted, the copy I have of Heart of Darkness[4] is a Dover Thrift Edition, which carries the whopping cover price of $1.50 … which means that the odds of it being in a brick-and-mortar (who might have a 60¢ mark-up on it) are fairly small, but both of the big on-line guys have this (heck, B&N even knocks another 10% off!), which is convenient for situations where you're getting a couple of books, and aren't *quite* at that $25 free-shipping level. If you like adventure books, or English Lit "classics", make a note of it and have it handy for the next time you're ordering on-line!

Notes:

1. http://btripp-books.livejournal.com/119654.html
2. http://amzn.to/1mOc47B
3. http://en.wikipedia.org/wiki/Apocalypse_Now
4. http://amzn.to/1mOc47B

Saturday, November 5, 2011[1]

The other side of the story ...

OK, so if you're following along, you'll realize that this is the second Dover Thrift Edtions book in a row ... aside from the benefits detailed in my previous review[2], these also tend to be short, and in months when I've either not been able to get a lot of reading (towards my annual target of 72 books) done, or have been stuck in a thick volume, jumping into these helps keep those numbers up! Frankly, I suspect that this is the first year since I've set that target that I'm not going to make it, unless I win the lottery or something and can clear my job-search schedule for some intense reading.

Anyway, this is another of those "how come I've never read that?" titles, that, while familiar, never got assigned in school, nor found its way into my reading pile (until it became a handy way to get free shipping on an on-line order). Of course, Frederick Douglass' Narrative of the Life of Frederick Douglass[3] is a sociological/historical classic, a first-person retelling of the author's life as a slave and his eventual life as a free man.

Douglass was fortunate to have been, as a lad, passed along to a family in Baltimore, where he was able to get a basis in reading ... largely teaching himself with the discarded work books of the family's children, and then passing along these skills to the poor *white* children in his area, with whom he shared many attributes.

One of the more surprising things in his experiences was how much he was passed around, as my view of slavery has been greatly flavored by films of the Civil War era, where it seemed that slaves were born, lived, and died on vast plantations, owned by the same families through generations. Douglass was in numerous situations before his escape.

The other feature here that amazed me was how openly hostile to religion he was. I don't know if the abolitionist organizations which he rose to fame with in New England were closely aligned with "free thinker" groups, but it is refreshing hearing passages along the lines of:

> "... Another advantage I gained in my new master was, he made no pretentions to, or profession of, religion; and this, in my opinion, was truly a great advantage. I assert most unhesitatingly, that the religion of the south is a mere covering for the most horrid crimes – a justifier of the most appalling barbarity, - a sanctifier of the most hateful frauds, - and a dark shelter under which the darkest, foulest, grossest, and most infernal deeds of slaveholders find the strongest protection. Were I to be again reduced to the chains of slavery, next to that en-

> slavement, I should regard being the slave of a religious master the greatest calamity that could befall me. For of all slaveholders with whom I have ever met, religious slaveholders are the worst. I have ever found them the meanest and basest, the most cruel and cowardly, of all others."

The book even closes with an Appendix directly addressing the links between Christianity and slavery, in which he continues:

> "... We see the thief preaching against theft, and the adulterer against adultery. We have men sold to build churches, women sold to support the gospel, and babes sold to purchase Bibles for the **poor heathen! All for the glory of God and the good of souls!** The slave auctioneer's bell and the church-going bell chime in with each other, and the bitter cries of the heart-broken slave are drowned in the religious shouts of his pious master. Revivals of religion and revivals in the slave-trade go hand in hand together. The slave prison and the church stand near each other. The clanking of fetters and the rattling of chains in the prison, and the pious psalm and solemn prayer in the church, may be heard at the same time. The dealers in the bodies and souls of men erect their stand in the presence of the pulpit, and they mutually help each other. The dealer gives his blood-stained gold to support the pulpit, and the pulpit, in return, covers his infernal business with the garb of Christianity. Here we have religion and robbery the allies of each other – devils dressed in angels' robes, and hell presenting the semblance of paradise."

> "... Dark and terrible as is this picture, I hold it to be strictly true of the overwhelming mass of professed Christians in America. They strain at a gnat, and swallow a camel. Could any thing be more true of our churches? They would be shocked at the proposition of fellowshipping a **sheep**-stealer; and at the same time they hug to their communion a **man**-stealer, and brand me with being an infidel, if I find fault with them for it. They attend with Pharisaical strictures to the outward forms of religion, and at the same time neglect the weightier matters of the law, judgment, mercy, and faith. They are always ready to sacrifice, but seldom to show mercy. They are they who are represented as professing to love God whom they have not seen, whilst they hate

> *their brother whom they have seen. They love the heathen on the other side of the globe. They can pray for him, pay money to have the Bible put into his hand, and missionaries to instruct him,; while they despise and totally neglect the heathen at their own doors."*

Needless to say, much of the sentiment here is *clearly* applicable in our own times, where the forces of religion push towards a theocratic dystopia. It's also hard to square Douglass' experience with the affiliations of American Blacks with both Christian and Muslim (the one who *ran* the slave trade) denominations.

Narrative of the Life of Frederick Douglass[4] should be a must-read for anybody unclear on the concept of slavery's history in the U.S., and is certainly an eye-opener for the connection of slavery and religious fundamentalism. While the Dover Thrift Edition may not be in your local brick-and-mortar, both of the on-line big boys have it, and with a $1.50 cover price (B&N has it at 10% off of *that*), its an ideal add-on for your next on-line order!

Notes:

1. http://btripp-books.livejournal.com/119992.html
2. http://btripp-books.livejournal.com/119654.html
3-4. http://amzn.to/1P0t2Wr

Sunday, November 6, 2011[1]

Kept waiting for them to call me "maggot" ...

This was another review copy sent to me by the good folks at Wiley, no doubt with the expectation that I'll be featuring the book in my The Job Stalker[2] blog over on the Tribune's "ChicagoNow" site. As much as I appreciate getting books from various publishers, I really would prefer to have a JOB rather than a "niche" writing about the Job Search ... it's been 2½ years now since my last regular gig disappeared, and it's getting desperate.

That level of desperation taints my impression of books such as Guerrilla Marketing for Job Hunters[3] by Jay Conrad Levinson and David E. Perry, as, almost inevitably, "step one" (or something close to "step one") is to define your "dream job" and work forward from that. Well, my dream job is "Billionaire Philanthropist" and I can't figure out where to send my resume for that. I am in my *third* major job search of the past decade or so, and I have been though workshops, coaching, dozens of on-line things, all sorts of group work, but I've never found a "career diagnostic" which has been able to point me to something focused enough to have the essential *"list of companies"* which "need" (or "have a pain" for which I'd be the specific relief) what I'm bringing to the table. Frankly, I have a wide and varied skill set within the "communications" field, and would be OK with working in any particular facet of that, but would really be happiest "wearing a lot of hats" and bringing my assorted skills to the fore in combination or rotation ... try making THAT fit the "company list" modality!

Anyway, pardon the rant. This book had me swearing at it at one moment, and being very enthusiastic about it the next. Your mileage may vary ... if you're the type who can identify exactly what you want to be doing, and then find a list of potential employers for whom you could perform that function, you're golden.

Guerrilla Marketing[4] is a dense book, covering a lot of material, and I guess I'll just walk you through this here. The intro and Chapter 1 pretty much set the stage (how dire things are now, why you need to do the extraordinary to get the job, etc.) for the Guerrilla job search. In here they say that the #1 secret to getting hired is *"Have a plan and follow it."*, with the #2 secret being *"Show an employer that your are worth much more to them than you cost."*

The book then moves to "Part I – Your Guerrilla Mind-Set", with chapters covering Personal Branding, Attitude, and Strategy. The "Personal Branding" involves a handful of key elements: Leadership Skills, Communication Skills, A Bias Toward Action, Passion, and Cultural Compatibility ... I've actually already implemented some of this in an application I put it for a position last week, going into a much more detailed cover letter than I normally would have. In "Attitude" there's a list of mistakes to avoid: #1 Fuzzy Goals, #2 Procrastination, #3 Relying on Others Too Much, #4 Lack of Preparation

… you can guess my reaction to the "fuzzy goals" section. In "Strategy" there are ways to tweak Google and Twitter to dig up a lot of information, and ways to get the most out of "traditional" job search sources.

One thing I should point out here is that each chapter has "guest pieces" by assorted Job industry pundits, including several who I follow on Twitter. These bring in "expert" voices on particular topics, and break up the flow of the book (which is a bit "drill instructor-ish" at times). It also has a LOT of those Mircosoft code blocks … I don't know about you, but the FIRST time that I both had the book and my phone together was when I sat down to write this review at a cafe, so I don't know how useful those really are (the one I just tested went to a YouTube video about using Google's advanced search capabilities). There are also "download available" icons through the book, but I've not run across the place which tells you where to go to retrieve them.

Anyway, this brings us to "Part II – Weapons That Make You A Guerrilla", which covers Research, Writing (resumes and cover letters), and Networking. "Research" looks at finding info on the industry, companies in that industry, and hiring managers at those companies, with tips, tricks, and assorted approaches to get this material. "Writing" is one of the more extensive sections here, as the authors are proposing some rather radical "Guerrilla Resume" formats and take a good while in justifying these. "Networking" details a gutsy cold-calling approach that utilizes a combination of Google and LinkedIn to find folks who have recently *left* your target company, with scripts to dig up information, etc.

Next is "Part III – Tactics That Make You A Guerrilla" with sections on LinkedIn, "Digital Breadcrumbs", and "Breakthrough Strategies". The authors are certainly fans of LinkedIn, and the chapter on it is chock-full of useful ways of maximizing this resource. "Digital Breadcrumbs" is all about using Social Media and the web in order to be found (or having the stuff *you* want to be found show up in a web search), this covers web portfolios, web sites, blogs, LinkedIn, Google, Facebook, Myspace, Twitter, video resumes, and a handful of sites I'd never heard of (but have run off to snag "BTRIPP" on!). In "Breakthrough Strategies" there are 15 listed, but they appear to come from a bigger list, as they're randomly in there, from "#5: The Coffee Cup Caper" to "#183: Distribute a Booklet", and cover a lot of ground from the plausible/evident to sneaky tactics like folding up your resume in a thank you note, which is far more likely to be opened by the target person.

Finally, there's "Part IV – Your Guerrilla Job-Hunting Campaign", with chapters on "The Force Multiplier Effect", "Interviewing", "Negotiating the Deal", and "Career Lancing". The first of these is pretty much just a collection of stories of various people who moved "outside the box" on things done in their job search, with suggestions of how you could do so as well. The "Interviewing" chapter (which is actually titled "Hand-to-Hand Combat"), talks about numerous types of interviews, ways to get past "trap" questions, and advice for getting interviewed "as far up the totem pole" as possible. "Negotiating the Deal" has a lot of hints about what to try to get, what not to bother with, and how to get things to "deal away" in final negotiations.

"Career Lancing" is just a coda encouraging readers to be always prepared for the job search.

[Guerrilla Marketing for Job Hunters](#)[5] just came out this summer, so it's likely to still be easy to find in your local bookstore, but both of the big on-line guys have it at 35% off of cover, which makes it quite reasonable (almost down to the cheapest current offer from the new/used guys). Despite my aggravation with the "anti-Fuzzy" bias, this is a remarkable resource for those who dare to break out of the ordinary job search.

Notes:

1. http://btripp-books.livejournal.com/120127.html
2. http://jobstalker.info/
3-5. http://amzn.to/1P0rH1Q

Tuesday, November 8, 2011[1]

Outside the norm ...

This is one of those books that I sort of knew the general outlines of, but had never quite ended up reading the text, so picked it up when I noticed it at a *deep* discount from the on-line guys. Obviously, Malcolm Gladwell has had a lot of very influential books, with titles (such as *The Tipping Point*) and assorted concepts working their way into the vernacular (or at least the punditsphere). I had, personally, stated to use this one's title (albeit in its statistical meaning) in my own conversations, and I figured that I should read Outliers: The Story of Success[2] just to make sure that some latter-day Inigo Montoya didn't end up telling me: *"You keep using that word. I do not think it means what you think it means."*!

Frankly, I'm amazed that books like *The Tipping Point* and *Outliers* sell the bazillion copies that they do, as they're hardly what I expect the unwashed fiction-readers of the world to venture into (holding to the George Carlin math about "how stupid the average person is") ... having been in the publishing biz, I wonder how things like Gladwell's books become memes working their way through the *Zeitgeist*, while hundreds of others don't even register (an interesting factoid: only a tiny fraction of books, about 2%, sell as many as 5,000 copies ... that's only 100 copies *per State* in the U.S. ... a fact which if I had in 1994, I'd probably never gone forward with my press!). I guess that Gladwell's bio (a former reporter with the Washington Post, and a long-time writer for *The New Yorker*) has presented him with opportunities and audience that most others lack.

That's actually one of the key elements here, "opportunity" ... it's a thread running through the "success" parts here (there are also non-success tales here), and the theme to Part One of the book (Part Two is "Legacy") ... although, interestingly, he doesn't raise the particulars of his publishing success here, despite having an auto-biographical study as the book's last chapter.

Outliers[3] is split into these two sections, with five chapters each, plus one in the introduction. They all deal somewhat with statistics, but also with cultural elements that persist well past when the initial impetus for behaviors (tied to cultural situations) have been left behind. This starts (in the introduction) with a look at a small town in Pennsylvania, which had been founded by Italian immigrants in the waning years of the 19th Century, mainly coming from a town of the same name in Italy. A doctor, vacationing in the area in the 1950's heard tell that nobody in Roseto, PA seemed to die of anything from old age. The doctor brought in a full research group and found that it wasn't their diet, it wasn't their genes, it wasn't their environment ... but it appeared to be their *culture*, which limited stress, and created all sorts of social webs of support, which was causing the remarkable lack of typical disease.

In subsequent chapters the author looks at Canadian hockey, and how the *birth dates* of kids in the developmental leagues determines who succeeds (the ones with birthdays closest to the cut-off dates end up older, more co-ordinated, and more trained than kids a few weeks on the other side of those registration deadlines), and how this "selection bias" affects other systems. Next he presents the "10,000 Hour Rule", which initially comes out of looking at classical musicians, and that the more practice they put in on their instrument, the better they are … with the threshold of excellence coming in at about 10,000 hours of practice. This then is expanded to look at people as divergent as Bill Joy (who wrote much of UNIX), Bill Gates, and The Beatles. The fact that both Joy and Gates had *opportunities* (outlined in the book) to use computer equipment *far* beyond the norm in their youth, and The Beatles had their "Hamburg Years" (when they played eight hours a day, seven days a week), that they became *better* at what they were doing than anybody else. This was then contrasted with an interesting analysis, similar to the hockey birthdate one, where it showed how out of the greatest fortunes (looking at the 75 richest people *in human history*, including Tsars, Pharaohs, and Emperors) almost one in five were amassed by a number of Americans born within a single decade, 1831-1840. And this, in turn is contrasted with the leading lights of the computer revolution, a remarkable number of whom were born from 1953-1956.

The next area the book looks at is "genius" and how being high-IQ is not necessarily a predictor of success, or at least if one is in a high-IQ group, having a higher IQ doesn't seem to help. As far as success goes, one just needs to be smart enough to get into a good school, *and make the most of that opportunity*.

From here the books looks at cultural influence … first with Jewish immigrants to the U.S., and how they made opportunities for themselves, based on long-established patterns of commerce from their situations in Europe. This then turns to the world of Law in New York, when Jewish lawyers would take the cases that the established firms wouldn't (corporate acquisitions, etc.), and were in place when the societal mood shifted to make this a major part of legal practice.

Culture becomes the central issue of the next couple of chapters, first looking at the attitudes of people coming from Kentucky, Tennessee, West Virginia, etc. with a story of a long-running feud between families, and how that related to the clan-based cultures of the Scottish highlands and the Scotts-Irish immigrants. Research at the University of Michigan showed that conditions set up to aggravate test subjects would have virtual *no* effect on those from Northern states, but would predictably produce anger reactions in the Southerners … although the subjects might be dozens of generations from their cultural roots as herdsmen.

A fascinating section follows called "The Ethnic Theory of Plane Crashes" which analyzes clusters of crashes from specific airlines (primarily South Korean and from South American countries), which deal with "Hofstede's Dimensions" which include such things as "uncertainty avoidance" (the tendency to stick to plans and procedures regardless of circumstances) and the "Power Distance Index" (indicative of how much deference a subordinate holds to his superiors). It turns out that most of these accidents were based on flight crew expressing their cultural norms (in one case the pilot *slapped* another officer for questioning his decision) and not taking the particulars of the situation to their logical conclusions (which would have required standing up to the pilot, or pressing the extreme nature of their problem with ground control). Not surprisingly, the "lowest" five countries on the PDI scale are the U.S., Ireland, South Africa, Australia, and New Zealand … all home to individualists with little respect for authority.

A similar "cultural" lens is turned to the subject of math competency and how Orientals seem to be better at math than most other cultures. Gladwell points to the cultivation of rice as creating a cultural modality for focused, around-the-calendar, work (as opposed to wheat cultivation, for example), and it is this, rather than innate competency which gives the Orientals a leg up. The next chapter looks at how a culture can form amid another, with the success of KIPP programs in the inner city, where, for those involved, it becomes a culture unto itself. The last chapter looks at the author's own history, going back to an Irish coffee plantation owner in Jamaica, and a pretty black slave he bought because of her looks … he details how various elements in the history of Jamaica and the Commonwealth, and some iron-willed ancestors of his, managed to create opportunities for his family.

Outliers[4] is a remarkable book, and should certainly be available from any of the better-stocked brick-and-mortar booksellers, but the on-line guys have it at about 1/3rd off cover, which makes it quite affordable.

Notes:

1. http://btripp-books.livejournal.com/120514.html

2-4. http://amzn.to/1P0pTFT

Tuesday, November 22, 2011

Not just for marketers ...

This was a strange sourcing ... I actually got queried by the folks at Wiley if I'd be interested in getting Ross Shafer's Grab More Market Share: How to Wrangle Business Away from Lazy Competitors[2] (frequently books just *arrive* these days), and I almost said "no" ... as you might surmise from the title/subtitle that this could well be a book for MBAs with iffy morals ("but I repeat myself"), which hardly fits in with the sort of business book I'd be interested in reading/reviewing, as much of that is targeted for my job-search blog, The Job Stalker[3], over on the Tribune's "ChicagoNow" site. I'm glad I said "yes", however, as this was entertaining, informative, and applicable in its details to much more to "grabbing more market share".

The book starts off very much in line with the title, talking about how McDonald's launched their McCafé a couple of years back, aiming to develop a *billion* dollars in new revenue. Putting the McCafé offerings in 11,000 of their 14,000 locations, McDonald's is already half way to their revenue goal, and in the same time Starbucks has closed several hundred locations. McDonald's didn't create a billion dollars in business, but saw where Starbucks was vulnerable and *stole* the traffic, initially with convenience, and then with dollar pricing ... even in the midst of the current recession/depression.

One of the concepts that Shafer pushes is "culture" ...

> The public, the culture the collective thinking of a lot of people also decide whether the goods and services you sell will become popular. If what you sell is popular, it is in demand. It becomes relevant and important to <u>them</u>. Your company will grow when <u>they</u> rush out and tell their friends.

However, he also points out that *"trends never sneak up on anybody"* and goes through a list of one-time category kings that fell because they couldn't adapt to the wants of the culture, while others (here, specifically Apple) built new empires by selling to those wants. Interestingly many of the failed companies had *developed* the technology that eventually killed them (such as Kodak and the digital camera), but never had the vision, or internal systems, to successfully meet the consumers' wants.

There's a lot in the middle of Grab More Market Share[4] about customer service, and "crowdsourcing", which certainly dovetails with much of the social media material (and experience) I've absorbed over the past several years, with practical suggestions (each chapter also has a "homework" section) for how to at least *conceptualize* these elements for one's business (and, as I noted above, this even had applicability for *the job search*, piquing my interest). He does push the limits a bit, highlighting Fred Reichheld's suggestion (from his *The Ultimate Question* book) that out *"of all the survey questions you can ask a customer, only one really matters: "How likely are you to recommend us to your friends?""*.

Again, this is targeted to business owners, but it's not a stretch in any of these chapters to be able to take the examples and the homework questions, and generate some really interesting ideas of *anybody's* situation. Shafer talks about developing "Trusted Advisors" as advocates for your brand and business, of "Contrarian Thinkers" (and how not all of us are crazy) with examples of how an auto paint manufacturer pulled scheduling systems from *wedding planners* to make the shift from oil-based paints to water-based paints practicable for their hundreds of paint-shop customers, how shooting for the "ultra luxury" niche seems to be a good bet for a lot of companies, and how, in a range of scenarios, companies with vision (or maybe just luck) managed to swallow up their competition:

> In Canada the lending laws still require home buyers to put a substantial amount of their own money down on a house – and to verify they have the income to afford the mortgage payment (Novel approach, isn't it?) Because of these controls, Toronto Dominion Bank sidestepped the toxic subprime mortgage market and has since gobbled up 1,000 bank branches from Maine to Florida.

Finally, the author takes a look an non-office working situations, and the hiring of the "older worker" (needless to say, from *my* perspective, this latter trend can't come on fast enough!). Having been blogging about job-search topics for the past two years, I'm surprised that I've not (as far as I can recall) run across the acronym ROWE – Results Only Work Environment ... maybe this is some new "MBA speak" that hasn't filtered down to creatives/communications folks. This came initially from two Best Buy employees, and has been implemented by Gap Outlet, as well as IBM, AT&T, and Sun Microsystems. ROWE generally involves workers on the other end of an electronic connection, with no schedules, no mandatory, meetings, and no "busy work". As long as the projects get done when they need to get done, the work can be done any time, and anywhere.

As far as hiring older workers, there are some interesting figures here ... *"with people over 55 almost twice as likely to launch successful companies than those between 20 and 34"* ... and thumbnails of successful recent start-ups by "more seasoned" folks, as well as companies that are pulling in the experienced workforce. If anybody out there is looking to jump on this trend ... I'm looking for work!

I have some slight caveats about [Grab More Market Share](#)[5], however. The first one is actually something that drew me to reading this (as I'm way behind on my 72-book annual reading target), and that this is *very* short, with the main body of the book is under 100 pages, with another 10 at the end with assorted URLs. And, speaking of that section, it seems rather unhelpful

... even as much as I've griped about books with QR codes in them heading off to web resources, having this mass of need-to-type links at the end seems so 2006. I'd have preferred them as footnotes or section end notes, so they'd be spread out across the book (and in context), but I guess this is one of those things that's always going to be an issue with dead-tree books interfacing with the Internet, and I fear that it will only be resolved on that sad day when books are things that you pull up on tablet devices. I was surprised that, after poking around on the web for a bit, there didn't seem to be a one-stop resource for these out there ... it would certainly be simple enough for the author to put these ten pages of links on a page on his web site, which would mean just typing the one URL and then clicking on the rest there!

Anyway, this was a good read, and I'm really glad that I told the folks at Wiley to send along a copy. While it is, as noted, very much "business owner" book (there's a section up front addressed to "Leaders" which rather blatantly pitches the author's speaking business!), it is structured in such a way that most of the material can be extrapolated to anybody's benefit. It's been out for only a month at this point, so the brick-and-mortar stores that carry business titles are likely to have it, but both of the big on-line guys have it at 27% off of retail (and, oddly, the used guys are *already* hawking copies), which makes it fairly reasonable (its cover price *is* a bit high for such a slim volume). As you can tell by the above, I found a lot of "new and interesting" material here, and you might like it too.

Notes:

1. http://btripp-books.livejournal.com/120820.html
2. http://amzn.to/1P0nVW0
3. http://jobstalker.info/
4-5. http://amzn.to/1P0nVW0

Sunday, November 27, 2011[1]

And, what IS reality?

As regular readers of this space know, I read quite a lot of Shamanic material, due, of course, to my having done a lot of traveling and study with various Shamanic teachers back in the 80's and 90's. As such, I have a fairly good "nose" for what is "fictionalized" and what tries to be a straight-forward presentation of the "reality" of a situation. A sample of the latter would be Joan Parisi Wilcox's Masters of the Living Energy[2], which is a very excellent book about the Q'ero, that rings true. An example of the former would be the early books of my own teacher, Alberto Villoldo, whose books covering times when I was with him in Peru have changed names, shuffled places, and a timeline nothing like what actually happened. Of course, the works of Castaneda are likewise largely "fictionalized", so Alberto's books are not unique in this aspect. At one point I heard Albert describe his writing method at the time as "dropping off a file box full of notebooks and random scraps of paper" to his writing partner, so it turns out that much of the "fictionalization" came from the unlucky wordsmith who had to patch together a coherent story line from such variable and disconnected materials!

I bring this up because Serge Kahili King's works, including Changing Reality[3] are frustrating to me because they both have *excellent* Shamanic material, but "iffy" backstories. I talked about this in the reviews of other "Huna" books I've done in the past few months, but it kept coming up in this. Detractors of Serge King have accused his "Hawaiian" Shamanism of being a mélange of other, non-native sources, ranging from Blavatsky to Gurdjieff to Shah ... and certainly materials resonating to those teachers do arise in much of his writing. However, the "core" experiential bits are very true to the general Shamanic experience. Of course, the "Shamanic experience" is (in my opinion) a universal base of spiritual experience, so a Shaman from Finland and a Shaman from the Amazon basin and a Shaman from the Pacific Northwest tribes will frequently have very similar experiences, filtered through cultural symbologies and environmental particulars, so saying that Huna "isn't like that" is hard to assert, especially given the insular nature of the Hawaiian culture. King claims that his teaching comes from an adoptive uncle, which (from what I've read in other books) would pretty much be the only way how a White Guy could connect with the nuts-and-bolts of the tradition. However, in Changing Reality[4] he attributes *teaching stories* to this uncle which are fairly well known ... in one case a Zen story, and, in another, a tale long presented as by Sufi character Mullah Nasruddin! While the "prankster" role of the Shamanic teacher is also quite common, one has to wonder why the author would take familiar stories from other traditions and claim them to be coming from the very uncle upon whose "native knowledge" his "Huna" tradition gets its "legitimacy"?

One of the elements key to the concepts of Changing Reality[5] is the idea of "levels of reality", with the Objective, the Subjective, the Symbolic, and the Holistic Worlds, each of which deals with experience in a different way. Much of the book walks through these levels of reality, with exercises and thought experiments, and stories from King's own work. Frankly, the flow of the book does seem like going through a week-long workshop, as the chapters build one on each other, with the basic concepts of the levels, and the main Huna ideas, being set out first, and then ESP, telepathy, and active aspects of telepathy, aura work, telekinesis, dream work, and astral travel added on as things progress.

In the later chapters King gets into "nature of reality" questions, and, while he doesn't ground these in specific "physics" theories, these certainly (for me, at least, having read a lot in this area as well) hang over the discussion. The "Copenhagen interpretation", and related many-worlds interpretations, as well as similar Multiverse theories, all seem to be in play here, if not specifically mentioned. His image of these overlapping realities is that of a ream or paper dumped out on a desk, with the individual sheets being a different reality, and that, with enough energy or focus, these can be traversed. A rather remarkable example he gives was when, on a trip, the cap of his toothpaste fell down the sink in a hotel bathroom, to which he loudly and energetically said "NO!" (or, I suspect some slightly more colorful outburst), at which point *"in the next moment I actually saw the cap re-materialize beside the drain that it had just gone into"*! Obviously, this is something which sounds like madness from the "Objective" world perspective, but becomes plausible if the action happens on one of the higher planes.

I felt the following section important enough to what King's getting at to re-type here for you:

> *This {changing the material world} should not be surprising, since we find evidence for this in all four worldviews. The Objective Level tells us that all matter is in a state of constant change. That what seems to be solid matter is actually mostly space, and that what little matter there is in that space is mostly composed of electrical charges and waves. The Subjective Level tells us that everything is energy, that everything is connected, and that mental energy changes emotional energy that changed physical energy. The Symbolic Level says that everything is a dream symbol, and that when one symbol changed, that changes all related symbols. The Holistic Level says that everything is one, and that when one thing changes, all things change. It is important to note that, while this book is concentrating on consciously-directed change, the carious worldviews assume that change can happen regardless of our conscious involvement.*

As noted above, there are exercises to do in every step here, so as "far out" as the material presented here is, you are at least able to do your own venture into "changing reality".

Again, I have my doubts about "Huna" as a tradition (at least extracted from its purported native context), but I have no doubts that what Serge Kahili King is presenting is a *system* which is organically Shamanic, and very powerful. I have found amazing things in all his books, and [Changing Reality][6] is certainly an example of this. Unfortunately, this is *also* an example of the hazards of a self-published (well, from King's [HunaWorks][7]) book. Aside from the lay-out (with evidently no attention being paid to "widows/orphans" on how the text flows page-to-page), there were *at least* a dozen typos that jumped off the page. Having been the editor-in-chief of a small publishing house, these sorts of things make me cringe, and really wish that King had spent the money to have a freelance editor (I just happen to know one) work with him on the production of the book. Usually when I think a book needs "editorial help", it's on content, but in the case of [Changing Reality][8], it's purely on a "cleaning it up" level (which could, also, included cover design).

Anyway, this is available through both of the on-line big boys, who each have it at the same 24% off of cover discount. The odds of finding it on the shelf of any other a metaphysical book store might be slim, given its provenance, but you could also order it direct. In any case, I (with the noted caveats) liked this very much, and would recommend it to anybody who "is into these things", or want to have their worldview shaken up a bit!

Notes:

1. http://btripp-books.livejournal.com/120936.html
2. http://btripp-books.livejournal.com/71456.html
3-6. http://amzn.to/1RuN4iz
7. http://www.huna.net/
8. http://amzn.to/1RuN4iz

Monday, November 28, 2011[1]

A "feel good" business book ...

I've been very fortunate that over the past 8 months running I've "won" something from LibraryThing.com's "Early Reviewer" program (I throw the quotes on "won" because, while it does have a competition aspect, with many more requesters than copies, the exchange of hours for the production/shipping cost of the book is more like volunteering to read/review a book for about 30¢/hour!), and this came to me from that source.

Blake Mycoskie is the founder of TOMS (which is a contraction of TOMorrow's Shoes), famed for giving away a pair to impoverished South American kids for every pair they sell, and Start Something That Matters[2] is *sort of* an autobiographical story of how he did that, and *sort of* an "inspirational" book for would-be entrepreneurs. For a book *sort of* targeted at would-be business owners, this is very "soft and gentle", going for a "feel good" level in the various stories presented here.

In 2006 he was in the midst of his *fourth* start-up, at the relatively tender age of 29. He ended up taking a vacation down to Argentina and both encountered the "national footwear" of a canvas shoe called the *alpargata*, and a charity group that was trying to get shoes for kids. These two elements cross-pollinated, and Mycoskie headed back to Los Angeles with a bag of the shoes, and an idea. Obviously, this took off as we're looking at the success (on both sides of the equation) of TOMS five years down the road.

Only the first chapter is specifically about the TOMS story (although elements of it come back in throughout the book), with the rest being Mycoskie's "business philosophy". To get an overview of this, here are the chapter titles: Find Your Story, Face Your Fears, Be Resourceful Without Resources, Keep It Simple, Build Trust, and Giving Is Good Business.

When I first started in on this review, I looked at all the bookmarks I'd put in and thought I'd have a bunch of copy blocks to put in here, but these were more "ideas" that I wanted to get back to. An example of these is where he talks about studies comparing the effectiveness of stories vs. facts. I've always been a big "facts guy", and it's unsettling to see how much more can be achieved with stories ... leading up to the point that *"Stories Resonate More Than Facts"* with a follow-up reminiscence of how a lady in an airport lounge launched into a massive rave about TOMS shoes *to him*, not realizing she was talking to their founder!

In "Face Your Fears", he recommends starting small (like his initial 250 pairs of shoes), so that you can build the story, and test the market, without big risks, and then make gradual improvements and expansions, while realizing *"The Timing Is Never Right"*.

It's also amazing how little they had in the early days, and how much they depended on unpaid interns (sourced from CraigsList), and had everybody working in the apartment he shared with other roommates, while said roomies were off at their day jobs! He has assorted suggestions for managing this sort of arrangement, and compares his experience with something like a dozen other start-ups.

He discusses other businesses all through the book, in some cases making them the main focus for a point, and in other to shed light on TOMS. In the "Giving" chapter he looks at various non-profits and for-profit operations that have a substantial charitable aspect to them.

The following is what he puts forward as part of the Keep It Simple chapter, the quick-and-dirty quiz for getting clear on what your business is about:

> THE SIMPLE PLAN
>
> Write <u>one</u> sentence to answer the questions below that pertain to what you are trying to do. For some of you, that could be all of them; for others, it might be just one:
>
> > 1) What is your business about?
> >
> > 2) What do you want to be known for as a person?
> >
> > 3) Why should someone hire you?
> >
> > 4) What social cause are you seeking to serve?
> >
> > 5) If you are designing a product or a service, look at it and then decide: What else can you remove from the design or service and still keep its function intact?
>
> The key is to answer the appropriate questions using a single sentence. If you can't then consider going back to the drawing board until you've honed your answers down to a simple statement.

Something tells me that the folks coming out of Wharton or Kellogg business schools would be confused by this (especially #4), but it sounded especially pithy to me. Of course, I've obviously not come up with a sufficiently compelling answer for #3, given my two and a half years of unemployment!

Start Something That Matters[3] just came out in September, so you're likely to be able to find copies in your local brick-and-mortar book source, but the on-line guys both have this at 39% off, so that's probably your best bet. This is addressed at potential business owners, but it was one of the more enjoyable "business" reads I've had in quite a while, so I'd really recommend it to "all and sundry" for it's "feel good" look at what is possible out there!

Notes:
1. http://btripp-books.livejournal.com/121268.html
2-3 http://amzn.to/1P0jxGs

Thursday, December 29, 2011[1]

So much depends on context ...

Here's another book that I got from LibraryThing.com's "Early Reviewer" program. Sam Sommers' Situations Matter: Understanding How Context Transforms Your World[2] is a fascinating look (as one might guess from the title/subtitle) at how the "frame" determines how one perceives the content of our experiences.

One of the key concepts Sommers uses here is that of "WYSIWYG", the acronym from the early days of graphical display of text on computer screens (and, yes, I do recall the days of the green or gold monochrome system display), "What You See Is What You Get". Obviously, it's been decades for most of us since this has been a concern, so I suppose that it's fair game for him to re-use, but (having lived through the evolution of text display) it seems somehow "off" in this context to me. Here's how he defines it:

> *The frame of social context has a similar impact on how people behave. When we overlook it, we produce an oversimplified picture of human nature, clinging as we do to the belief that <u>what you see is what you get</u>. Computer programmers ... [used] ... this phrase ... to refer to an interface that allows the user to see what the final product will look like while a document is being created. In daily life, even when we should know better, we endorse this idea of WYSIWYG ... when we assume that the behavior we observe of another person at a particular point in time provides an accurate glimpse of the "true product" within.*

The book is chock full of examples and studies which show people reacting to situations based on surface impressions, starting with one that shows that in a questioner/contestant situation, participants in a study rated the questioner 82 while rating the contestant 49, because the one asking the questions just seems that much smarter (and further illustrated by a thought experiment about which TV host one would want to hire as a tutor, Alex Trebek, Pat Sajak, or Ryan Seacrest). Similar dynamics are at play with "celebrity endorsers", were we to *think* about it, we'd realize that there is no special insight that the endorser has (beyond "endorsing" the advertiser's check) but their familiarity leads us to lend credence to the pitch.

The first major category that Sommers addresses here is that of crowds ... the more people observing a situation, the less likely any of those people are to act ... *"When no one in the crowd seems concerned by what's gong on, each of us feels more comfortable with the status quo, contributing to a cycle of inaction that only continues as new individuals enter the scene."* ...

he concludes with a suggestion that in an emergency the best approach to get assistance is to specifically single out an individual to ask for help. From the passive inertia of crowds Situations Matter[3] turns to the active role of conforming in various situations, from the shills whose role is to work up crowds at sporting events (there is a whole profession dedicated to this) to the function of social exchange. Frankly, some of the numbers here are mind-blowing, but various studies have shown that participants in experiments where actors were intentionally choosing wrong answers, *seventy five percent* of subjects would go against their senses at least once to be in agreement with the group! This is influenced by the reality that a group of people are likely to be, in the long run, more accurate in their responses than any given individual, but is surprising how big a lure conforming appears to be. A more common expression of this is in "reciprocity", where a charity sends along some token "gift" to increase giving, or a car salesman knocks some small percentage off a very overpriced option to help insure the sale. Another amazing number here is that in one study 93% of subjects complied with an inconvenient request when a meaningless "reason" was given ... only one percent less than what a reasonable request elicited (and well above the 60% compliance of just a request was made without a reason). Various situations are looked at here, Heaven's Gate, the People's Temple, Abu Gharib, and the notorious Milgram studies (where the presence of an "authority figure" increased compliance from 3% to 65%!), on to studies of how many extra pieces of candy trick-or-treaters would take in a group vs. alone.

The next part of the book looks at one's sense of self, and, again, there are amazing studies which show how context-dependent our view of who we are and what we believe and what we want are ...

> *Why is your sense of self so variable across situations?*
>
> *Because it depends, in large part, on who's around you and the culture in which you grew up. Because the process of introspection produces but a temporary snapshot of how you feel in this fleeting time and place.*

Add to this the rather bizarre factoid (based largely on the author's own research) that something like 85% of any group will rate themselves as "above average" on a given topic, which he notes is "a mathematical absurdity". Stranger still are the studies of people "preferring" letters from a random assortment which appear in their names, and the disproportionate number of people who live places that have names similar to their own, or even go into *professions* which are homophonic (i.e., "Larrys" becoming Lawyers).

> *Like the better-than-average effect, these surprising name-related findings reflect a propensity for seeing the world in an ego-enhancing light. Such self-serving tendencies are particularly likely when*

> we're confronted with our own shortcomings and failures. Indeed, we have an entire toolbox of strategies that we use to maintain positive self-regard in the face of the humbling and threatening experiences that constitute daily life ...

Next is a look at how expectation affects results, where those whose belief is that they're "set" at a particular level won't be as likely to go for self-improvement, which dovetails into gender issues and how pervasive preconceptions along these lines are in society. This then moves into the subject of "love", with somewhat ironic reflections on how proximity and familiarity are the most reliable gauges for attraction ... but also how reciprocity, obstacles, danger, and similarity come into play. From "love" the book moves to "hate" and looks how easily sides are taken in almost any situation, which then significantly influences further decision making in terms of bigotry and even militancy.

Needless to say, Situations Matter[4] is an interesting read, but it's also lively and engaging, with Sommers bringing in numerous personal stories amid the multitude of anecdotes of research studies regarding people's responses to various contextual settings. This is officially just coming out this week, so is likely to be appearing in your local brick-and-mortar book vendor, but both of the on-line big boys have it at 34% off of cover, which would be your best deal at this point.

Notes:

1. http://btripp-books.livejournal.com/121487.html

2-4. http://amzn.to/1OcsLIR

Saturday, December 31, 2011[1]

A splendid book ...

This was one of those "throw ins" that I'd seen on-line and added to an Amazon order ... with my only vaguely being aware of what it was about (i.e., I'd not seen a review, or had it recommended or followed up on a reference in another book). I'm very glad that I picked it up, as Jacob Needleman's What Is God?[2] is a really fantastic book. Those who follow me over on LibraryThing.com will appreciate this ... I actually *rated* it ... which I've only done on *four* books out of the over 2,000 I have over there!

Of course, there has to be a reason for this, and I think the surprise of stumbling over an unsuspected "Fourth Way" book has a lot to do with it. As folks who are familiar with my library know, I've read a lot in the Gurdjieff/Ouspensky oeuvre and I was rather pleasantly surprised to find that this is in that vein. However, this is not a book *about* that philosophy, but about the author's own path, which eventually finds its way *to* The Work.

What Is God?[3] is in four parts, dealing with various aspects of Needleman's search. It starts with his family, and his Jewish background, moves into his shift into Atheism, and encounters with Zen (especially a youthful, yet lasting in its effects, interaction with D.T. Suzuki), and various other religious traditions. He is a college professor by trade, and he looks at the way that has brought him to understand certain truths about people (students), and caused him to dig deeply into the inner workings of Christianity, Judaism, Gnosticism, etc. It was this latter influence that led him to the Gurdjieff material, and he approaches it with a very new awareness/perspective than any of the other books I've encountered on that. Interestingly, the book that grabbed him was one I've recently looked at here, the DeHartmanns' Our Life with Mr. Gurdjieff[4].

The second section follows his path further, his involvement with the Gurdjieff Society, his friendship with Tibetan teacher Lobsang Lhalungpa (who has a wonderful response to Needleman's question *"How can you say that it's rare to be born as a human being?"* while walking on a crowded San Francisco street, asking in return: *"How many human beings do you see?"*), and revisiting an early infatuation with Kant. Needless to say, this develops a heady mix of influences, world views, and approaches, which carries him into the third section, where he addresses a time in his courses when he, from an Atheistic point of view, had to deal with a student's Christian fundamentalism, and the *emotional* impact of religion, as unfolded via a discussion of William James' work, which leads him (and his class) to a sense of a "common ground" of all religions.

The final part deals with his eventual immersion with the Gurdjieff community ... I was very excited to read this, as I'd not suspected that there *was* any such thing, and was pleased to find out about the likes of Pentland and the on-going propagation of The Work (including finding out that there was a Gurdjieff Foundation of Illinois operating in Chicago!) ... and introducing his take on "attention":

> <u>I am my attention.</u> Everything else is given, is not mine. But what, exactly, is this uniquely human capacity which I do not understand or really value? I value something I call my knowledge, my skills, my actions; I feel remorse also for my actions, or feel pleased by them; I admire or dislike my body, my strength or weakness. But my attention? It <u>is I</u>! How could I fail to value it? How could I have lived without consciously recognizing it as the heart of what I am, the mind of what I am?

{I was struck by how this dove-tails with the current concept of *attention* in the Social Media sphere ... that what *counts* "out there" *is* attention, and here the concept comes up on the *inner planes* as well ... a sign of the singularity?} Needleman outlines moments of clarity in these contexts, and beautifully wraps them in the trappings of all his professorial data. The closing pages were so rich in important material that I had a bookmark stuck between nearly every one ... here are some key bits:

> ... we are on the verge of saying, knowing, the shocking truth that God needs not just man, but <u>awakened man</u>, in order to act as God in the human world. Without this conscious energy on the earth it may not be possible for diving justice, mercy, or compassion to enter the lives of human beings.

> ... a universe of intermediate beings between God and Man and between Man and Hell is rooted in inward experience – the age-old experience of life as a guided path, a way handed down in ever new language from ancient times to the present moment. There is the idea of a path, an inner work, leading step by step to the ability to receive "what the religions call God". And there is help at every step, from others whose essence-obligation is to transmit the Way to those who come after them. This aspect of religion has been largely forgotten in the West – it is only now just beginning to emerge again out of the shadows of the symbolic language that has not been received inwardly as the promise and the vision of inner evidence and proof of what we are and are meant to be.

> Man must choose; that power and gift is his essence. And the instrument, the principle instrument

> *of his choice is his uniquely human attention. But as he is now, man on earth is a being without Attention. His body, the cells and tissues of his body obey only the attention of the animal or the plant or the mineral within him. Man's being, as he is now, cannot obey his mind; it is his mind that obeys his body, which is of the animal or the plant or the mineral.*

Again, What Is God?[5] is not a book *about* theology, or philosophy, or The Work, but a wonderful telling of the author's journey of discovery. As noted at the start here, I found this particularly awesome, and I'd recommend it to *anybody*, but especially to anyone who is a "searcher" or has an interest in the Fourth Way materials. It has only been out for a couple of years, so should be "out there", but the on-line guys have it for 35% off of cover, and there are copies in the used channels for a low as a penny (plus shipping). Make sure to pick this one up … it's a treasure!

Notes:

1. http://btripp-books.livejournal.com/121717.html

2-3. http://amzn.to/1PY0UYV

4. http://btripp-books.livejournal.com/117938.html

5. http://amzn.to/1PY0UYV

QR code links
to the
on-line reviews:

Switch: How to Change Things
When Change Is Hard
by
Chip & Dan Heath

The Seat of the Soul
by
Gary Zukav

Gunga Din and Other Favorite Poems
by
Rudyard Kipling

Content Rules: How to Create Killer Blogs,
Podcasts, Videos, Ebooks, Webinars (and More)
That Engage Customers and Ignite Your Business
by
Ann Handley & C.C. Chapman

The Imperial Cruise:
A Secret History of Empire and War
by
James Bradley

Real-Time Marketing and PR: How to Instantly
Engage Your Market, Connect with Customers,
and Create Products that Grow Your Business Now
by
David Meerman Scott

Cracking the Hidden Job Market:
How to Find Opportunity in Any Economy
by
Donald Asher

Realm of the Incas
by
Victor W. Von Hagen

Genesis of the Grail Kings
by
Laurence Gardner

What Color Is Your Parachute?
Job-Hunter's Workbook
by
Richard N. Bolles

The Importance of Being Earnest
by
Oscar Wilde

The Thank You Economy
by
Gary Vaynerchuk

The Invisible Touch:
The Four Keys to Modern Marketing
by
Harry Beckwith

Zen Buddhism, An Introduction to Zen with Stories,
Parables and Koan Riddles of the Zen Masters,
Decorated with Figures from Old Chinese Ink-Paintings
by
Peter Pauper Press

Purple Cow:
Transform Your Business by Being Remarkable
by
Seth Godin

The Twelfth Insight: The Hour of Decision
by
James Redfield

The NOW Revolution:
7 Shifts to Make Your Business Faster,
Smarter and More Social
by
Amber Naslund & Jay Baer

On the Hunt: How to Wake Up Washington
and Win the War on Terror
by
Col. David Hunt

50 Jobs in 50 States:
One Man's Journey of Discovery Across America
by
Daniel Seddiqui

An Open Heart:
Practicing Compassion in Everyday Life
by
His Holiness the Dalai Lama

The Entrepreneur Equation:
Evaluating the Realities, Risks, and Rewards
of Having Your Own Business
by
Carol Roth

Kahuna Magic
by
Brad Steiger

Synchronicity: An Acausal Connecting Principle
by
C.G. Jung

How Companies Win:
Profiting from Demand-Driven Business Models
No Matter What Business You're In
by
Rick Kash & David Calhoun

Sinagua Sunwatchers:
An Archaeoastronomy Survey
of the Sacred Mountain Basin
by
Kenneth J. Zoll

Iran, The Green Movement and the USA:
The Fox and the Paradox
by
Hamid Dabashi

A New Earth:
Awakening to Your Life's Purpose
by
Eckhart Tolle

Courageous Dreaming:
How Shamans Dream the World into Being
by
Alberto Villoldo

Jaguars Ripped My Flesh
by
Tim Cahill

Cities of the Maya in Seven Epochs,
1250 B.C. to A.D. 1903
by
Steve Glassman & Armando Anaya

What Color Is Your Parachute? Guide to Job-Hunting Online,
Sixth Edition: Blogging, Career Sites, Gateways, Getting Interviews,
Job Boards, Job Search Engines, Personal Websites, Posting Resumes,
Research Sites, Social Networking
by
Mark Emery Bolles

The Moral Landscape:
How Science Can Determine Human Values
by
Sam Harris

A History of PI
by
Petr Beckmann

Huna: Ancient Hawaiian Secrets for Modern Living
by
Serge Kahili King

The Plan of Chicago:
Daniel Burnham and the Remaking of
the American City
by
Carl Smith

Secret of the Forest:
On the Track of the Maya and Their Temples
by
Wolfgang Cordan

The Cluetrain Manifesto:
The End of Business as Usual
by
Rick Levine, Christopher Locke,
Doc Searls, & David Weinberger

The Human Genome:
Book of Essential Knowledge
by
John Quackenbush

The Celestine Vision:
Living the New Spiritual Awareness
by
James Redfield

Demystifying Tibet:
Unlocking the Secrets of the Land of the Snows
by
Lee Feigon

Surviving Your Serengeti:
7 Skills to Master Business and Life
by
Stefan Swanepoel

What Sticks: Why Most Advertising Fails
and How to Guarantee Yours Succeeds
by
Rex Briggs & Greg Stuart

The Seed:
Finding Purpose and Happiness in Life and Work
by
Jon Gordon

Keeper of Genesis:
A Quest for the Hidden Legacy of Mankind
by
Robert Bauval & Graham Hancock

Marketing Shortcuts for the Self-Employed:
Leverage Resources, Establish Online Credibility
and Crush Your Competition
by
Patrick Schwerdtfeger

W. B. Yeats: Selected Poems
by
William Butler Yeats

Dave Barry's History of the Millennium (So Far)
by
Dave Barry

Beyond the Da Vinci Code:
From the Rose Line to the Bloodline
by
Sangeet Duchane

101 Weird Ways to Make Money:
Cricket Farming, Repossessing Cars, and Other
Jobs With Big Upside and Not Much Competition
by
Steve Gillman

Beyond the Stream of the World
by
Phra Acariya Thoon Khippapañño

The Pearl of Great Price
by
Joseph Smith

Our Life with Mr. Gurdjieff
by
Thomas & Olga de Hartmann

Going Pro: How to Make the Leap
from Aspiring to Professional Photographer
by
Scott Bourne & Skip Cohen

Rhetoric and Kairos:
Essays in History, Theory, and Praxis
by
Phillip Sipiora & James S. Baumlin

God, No!:
Signs You May Already Be an Atheist
and Other Magical Tales
by
Penn Jillette

The Man of Numbers:
Fibonacci's Arithmetic Revolution
by
Keith Devlin

Japanese Religion, Unity and Diversity
by
H. Byron Earhart

The Master Key to Riches
by
Napoleon Hill

Heart of Darkness
by
Joseph Conrad

Narrative of the Life of Frederick Douglass
by
Frederick Douglass

Guerrilla Marketing for Job Hunters
by
Jay Conrad Levinson & David E. Perry

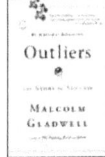

Outliers: The Story of Success
by
Malcolm Gladwell

Grab More Market Share:
How to Wrangle Business Away
from Lazy Competitors
by
Ross Shafer

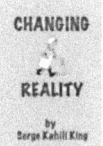

Changing Reality
by
Serge Kahili King

Start Something That Matters
by
Blake Mycoskie

Situations Matter:
Understanding How Context Transforms Your World
by
Sam Sommers

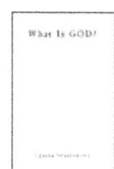

What Is God?
by
Jacob Needleman

CONTENTS - ALPHABETICAL BY AUTHOR

Donald Asher *Cracking the Hidden Job Market*	page	13
Jay Baer & Amber Naslund *The NOW Revolution*	page	37
Dave Barry *Dave Barry's History of the Millennium (So Far)*	page	109
Robert Bauval & Graham Hancock *Keeper of Genesis*	page	102
Petr Beckmann *A History of Pi*	page	76
Harry Beckwith *The Invisible Touch*	page	28
Mark Emery Bolles & Richard N. Bolles *What Color Is Your Parachute? Guide to Job-Hunting Online*	page	71
Richard N. Bolles *What Color Is Your Parachute? Job-Hunter's Workbook*	page	20
Scott Bourne & Skip Cohen *Going Pro*	page	123
James Bradley *The Imperial Cruise*	page	9
Rex Briggs & Greg Stuart *What Sticks*	page	98
Tim Cahill *Jaguars Ripped My Flesh*	page	66
Joseph Conrad *Heart of Darkness*	page	136
Wolfgang Cordan *Secret of the Forest*	page	83
Hamid Dabashi *Iran, The Green Movement and the USA*	page	59

His Holiness the Dalai Lama — page 46
An Open Heart

Thomas de Hartmann & Olga de Hartmann — page 120
Our Life with Mr. Gurdjieff

Keith Devlin — page 129
The Man of Numbers

Frederick Douglass — page 138
Narrative of the Life of Frederick Douglass

Sangeet Duchane — page 111
Beyond the Da Vinci Code

H. Byron Earhart — page 131
Japanese Religion, Unity and Diversity

Lee Feigon — page 93
Demystifying Tibet

Laurence Gardner — page 17
Genesis of the Grail Kings

Steve Gillman — page 113
101 Weird Ways to Make Money

Malcolm Gladwell — page 144
Outliers

Steve Glassman & Armando Anaya — page 68
Cities of the Maya in Seven Epochs, 1250 B.C. to A.D. 190

Seth Godin — page 32
Purple Cow

Jon Gordon — page 100
The Seed

Ann Handley & C.C. Chapman — page 7
Content Rules

Sam Harris — page 73
The Moral Landscape

Chip Heath & Dan Heath — page 1
Switch

Napoleon Hill *The Master Key to Riches*	page	133
Col. David Hunt *On the Hunt*	page	40
Penn Jillette *God, No!*	page	127
C.G. Jung *Synchronicity*	page	53
Rick Kash & David Calhoun *How Companies Win*	page	55
Phra Ācariya Thoon Khippapañño *Beyond the Stream of the World*	page	115
Serge Kahili King *Changing Reality*	page	150
Serge Kahili King *Huna*	page	79
Rudyard Kipling *Gunga Din and Other Favorite Poems*	page	5
Rick Levine, Christopher Locke, Doc Searls, David Weinberger *The Cluetrain Manifesto*	page	86
Jay Conrad Levinson & David E. Perry *Guerrilla Marketing for Job Hunters*	page	141
Blake Mycoskie *Start Something That Matters*	page	153
Jacob Needleman *What Is God?*	page	158
Peter Pauper Press *Zen Buddhism*	page	30
John Quackenbush *The Human Genome*	page	89
James Redfield *The Celestine Vision*	page	91

James Redfield *The Twelfth Insight*	page	34
Carol Roth *The Entrepreneur Equation*	page	48
Patrick Schwerdtfeger *Marketing Shortcuts for the Self-Employed*	page	104
David Meerman Scott *Real-Time Marketing and PR*	page	11
Daniel Seddiqui *50 Jobs in 50 States*	page	43
Ross Shafer *Grab More Market Share*	page	147
Phillip Sipiora & James S. Baumlin *Rhetoric and Kairos*	page	125
Carl Smith *The Plan of Chicago*	page	81
Joseph Smith *The Pearl of Great Price*	page	117
Sam Sommers *Situations Matter*	page	155
Brad Steiger *Kahuna Magic*	page	51
Stefan Swanepoel *Surviving Your Serengeti*	page	96
Eckhart Tolle *A New Earth*	page	61
Gary Vaynerchuk *The Thank You Economy*	page	25
Alberto Villoldo *Courageous Dreaming*	page	64
Victor W. Von Hagen *Realm of the Incas*	page	15

Oscar Wilde	page	23
The Importance of Being Earnest		
William Butler Yeats	page	107
W. B. Yeats: Selected Poems		
Kenneth J. Zoll	page	57
Sinagua Sunwatchers		
Gary Zukav	page	3
The Seat of the Soul		

CONTENTS - ALPHABETICAL BY TITLE

101 Weird Ways to Make Money
Steve Gillman   page   113

50 Jobs in 50 States
Daniel Seddiqui   page   43

Beyond the Da Vinci Code
Sangeet Duchane   page   111

Beyond the Stream of the World
Phra Ācariya Thoon Khippapañño   page   115

The Celestine Vision
James Redfield   page   91

Changing Reality
Serge Kahili King   page   150

Cities of the Maya in Seven Epochs, 1250 B.C. to A.D. 190
Steve Glassman & Armando Anaya   page   68

The Cluetrain Manifesto
Rick Levine, Christopher Locke, Doc Searls, David Weinberger   page   86

Content Rules
Ann Handley & C.C. Chapman   page   7

Courageous Dreaming
Alberto Villoldo   page   64

Cracking the Hidden Job Market
Donald Asher   page   13

Dave Barry's History of the Millennium (So Far)
Dave Barry   page   109

Demystifying Tibet
Lee Feigon   page   93

The Entrepreneur Equation
Carol Roth   page   48

Genesis of the Grail Kings
Laurence Gardner   page   17

Title	Author	Page
God, No!	Penn Jillette	127
Going Pro	Scott Bourne & Skip Cohen	123
Grab More Market Share	Ross Shafer	147
Guerrilla Marketing for Job Hunters	Jay Conrad Levinson & David E. Perry	141
Gunga Din and Other Favorite Poems	Rudyard Kipling	5
Heart of Darkness	Joseph Conrad	136
A History of Pi	Petr Beckmann	76
How Companies Win	Rick Kash & David Calhoun	55
The Human Genome	John Quackenbush	89
Huna	Serge Kahili King	79
The Imperial Cruise	James Bradley	9
The Importance of Being Earnest	Oscar Wilde	23
The Invisible Touch	Harry Beckwith	28
Iran, The Green Movement and the USA	Hamid Dabashi	59
Jaguars Ripped My Flesh	Tim Cahill	66
Japanese Religion, Unity and Diversity	H. Byron Earhart	131

Kahuna Magic
Brad Steiger   page   51

Keeper of Genesis
Robert Bauval & Graham Hancock   page   102

The Man of Numbers
Keith Devlin   page   129

Marketing Shortcuts for the Self-Employed
Patrick Schwerdtfeger   page   104

*The Master Key to Riche*s
Napoleon Hill   page   133

The Moral Landscape
Sam Harris   page   73

Narrative of the Life of Frederick Douglass
Frederick Douglass   page   138

A New Earth
Eckhart Tolle   page   61

The NOW Revolution
Jay Baer & Amber Naslund   page   37

On the Hunt
Col. David Hunt   page   40

An Open Heart
His Holiness the Dalai Lama   page   46

Our Life with Mr. Gurdjieff
Thomas de Hartmann & Olga de Hartmann   page   120

Outliers
Malcolm Gladwell   page   144

The Pearl of Great Price
Joseph Smith   page   117

The Plan of Chicago
Carl Smith   page   81

Purple Cow
Seth Godin   page   32

Title	Author	Page
Realm of the Incas	Victor W. Von Hagen	15
Real-Time Marketing and PR	David Meerman Scott	11
Rhetoric and Kairos	Phillip Sipiora & James S. Baumlin	125
The Seat of the Soul	Gary Zukav	3
Secret of the Forest	Wolfgang Cordan	83
The Seed	Jon Gordon	100
Sinagua Sunwatchers	Kenneth J. Zoll	57
Situations Matter	Sam Sommers	155
Start Something That Matters	Blake Mycoskie	153
Surviving Your Serengeti	Stefan Swanepoel	96
Switch	Chip Heath & Dan Heath	1
Synchronicity	C.G. Jung	53
The Thank You Economy	Gary Vaynerchuk	25
The Twelfth Insight	James Redfield	34
W. B. Yeats: Selected Poems	William Butler Yeats	107
What Color Is Your Parachute? Guide to Job-Hunting Online	Mark Emery Bolles & Richard N. Bolles	71

What Color Is Your Parachute? Job-Hunter's Workbook
Richard N. Bolles page 20

What Is God?
Jacob Needleman page 158

What Sticks
Rex Briggs & Greg Stuart page 98

Zen Buddhism
Peter Pauper Press page 30

www.ingramcontent.com/pod-product-compliance
Lightning Source LLC
Chambersburg PA
CBHW060519100426
42743CB00009B/1376